Out Of The Cage

by Alex McSweeney

Published by Playdead Press 2015

© Alex McSweeney 2015

Alex McSweeney has asserted his rights under the Copyright, Design and Patents Act, 1988, to be identified as the author of this work.

A CIP catalogue record for this book is available from the British Library.

ISBN 978-1-910067-30-7

Printed by BPUK

Playdead Press
www.playdeadpress.com

For Rachel

Following development at the IYAF Festival at The Rose Theatre Kingston in July 2014, *Out Of The Cage* was first performed at the Park Theatre on 20th January 2015 with the following cast:

Heather Bleasdale | Ol' Mum
Milly Finch | Jane Byass
Lindsay Fraser | Carrie Sefton
Tegen Hitchens | Dee Jessop
Emily Houghton | Annie Castledine
Sarah Madigan | Nelly Johnson
Jill McAusland | Lil' Ginny
Katherine Tozer | Nancy Longdon

Creative Team

Alex McSweeney | Playwright / Director
James Perkins | Designer
Gary Bowman | Lighting Designer
John Chambers | Composer and Sound Designer
Simon Pittman | Movement Director
Jane Arnold-Forster | Production Manager
Maeve Bolgar | Company Stage Manager
Alicia Bloundele | Assistant Director / Costume Supervisor
Kamila Gorecka | Design Assistant
Dan Street | Production Electrician / Programmer
Mobius Industries | Marketing
Alexander Milward at Kate Morley PR | Public Relations
Fine Line Productions | Producer
Robyn Keynes | Associate Producer

With thanks to Arts Council England, Legasee, Park Theatre, Stage One, St Martins Church Kensal Green, Rose Theatre Kingston, Martin Bisiker, Matthew Cullum, John Fairbairn, Alison and John Fraser, Paul Gavin of Purple Sheep, David Ottley, Elliot Robinson and Playdead Press, Dominic McSweeney and Jan Weekes of Weekes Brothers and Welling Ltd.

Heather Bleasdale | Ol' Mum
Trained at Drama Studio London.
Theatre includes: *When Five Years
Pass* (Fringe First, BAC); *Victory
Morning* (Bridewell); *Amy's View*
(National Theatre/West End u/s
played role); *The Weir* (Royal
Court u/s) and *Hungry* (UK tour).
TV includes: *Law & Order*; *Waking
the Dead*; *Silent Witness*; *Sons & Lovers*; *Casualty*;
Outnumbered; *Merseybeat*; *Warriors*; *Drop the Dead Donkey*;
Grafters; *Heartbeat*; *Eastenders*; *The Royal*; Secret *Diary of a
Callgirl*; *Murderland* and *Coronation Street*.
Film includes: *Last Chance Harvey*; *The Glasshouse* and
Harry Potter and the Chamber of Secrets.
Radio: *BBC Radio 4 Afternoon Plays*.

Milly Finch | Jane Byass
Trained at Webber Douglas.
Theatre includes: *Three Tall
Women* (Wyndham's Theatre);
Wuthering Heights (Rendlesham
Forest Theatre); *Blood Bath* (The
New Wolsey); *Robin Hood*; *Wind in
the Willows* (Norwich Playhouse)
and *The Sword in the Stone*
(Cambridge Arts Theatre).

Television and Film includes: *Our Tune*; *Agony*; *Crime
Watch Special*; *Soldier Boy* and *The Good Doctor*.

Lindsay Fraser | Carrie Sefton
Trained at East 15 Acting School.
Theatre includes: *Execution Of Justice* (Southwark Playhouse); *Just So Stories* (The Kings Head) and *Oh Go My Man* (Tristan Bates).
Film includes: *Touch* (Virgin Media Shorts winner); *Still Waters* (Memoir Pictures); *In Control*; *Hard Light* and *Cygnus*.

Tegen Hitchens | Dee Jessop
Theatre includes: *Bitesize Breakfast* (Pleasance, Edinburgh); *Lunchtime Fourplay* (St James); *New World Order* (Hydrocracker); *Accrington Pals* (The Old Market); *The Positive Hour* (Jermyn Street); *A Midsummer Night's Dream*; *The Caucasian Chalk Circle* (Drum

Theatre Royal Plymouth) and *The Musicians* (National Theatre).
Television and Film includes: *Easy Hours* (Film 4 Virgin Media Shorts) and *Michael* (BFI).

Emily Houghton | Annie Castledine
Trained at RADA.
Theatre includes: *Price of Money* (Belarus Free Theatre); *Much Ado About Nothing* (Ludlow Festival); *Angus, Thongs and Even More Snogging* (West Yorkshire Playhouse); *Dinnerladies* (UK Tour); *All My Sons* (Leicester Curve); *The Rape Of Lucrece* (Shakespeare's Globe) and *Thunderer* (Edinburgh Festival).
Television includes: *Lewis* (ITV); *Threesome* (Big Talk Productions) and *Doctors* (BBC).
Film includes: *Red Reflections* (Cannes 2014) and *Curtain* (Garden Gate Films).

Sarah Madigan | Nelly Johnson
Trained at LAMDA.
Theatre includes: *Old Habits* (Courting Drama/Southwark Playhouse); *The Notorious Mrs. Ebbsmith* (Jermyn Street Theatre); *Duck* (rehearsed reading for Out of Joint); *Celebration* (Gate Theatre,  Dublin) and *Measure for Measure* (Cockpit Theatre).
Television includes: *Marú* and *Saor Sinn Ó Olc* (TG4).
Film includes: *V.P* (Take Cover Films) and *Gingerbread Men* (Second Wave Films).

Jill McAusland | Lil' Ginny
Trained at Rose Bruford.
Theatre includes: *Sleeping
Beauty*; *Robin Hood*; *Mother
Goose* (Watford Palace
Theatre); *Ghost Town* (Pilot
Theatre, York Theatre Royal); *On
Reflection: Body Gossip Live* (Body
Gossip, Southbank
Centre); *Jumpy* (Royal Court West End, Duke of
York's); *Alice in Wonderland* (Northampton Theatre
Royal); *The Conspirators* (Orange Tree) and *The
Fumidor* (Pants On Fire, Kingston IYAF).
Television includes: *Doctors* and *Holby City* (BBC).

Katherine Tozer | Nancy Longdon
Theatre includes: *Hedda Gabler*
(London tour); *The House of
Bernarda Alba*; *A Streetcar Named
Desire* – TMA Nomination: Best
Actor (Nuffield Theatre
Southampton); *Hippolytus*
(Riverside Studios); *The Canterbury
Tales* (RSC); *Scapino*; *The Scarlet*

Letter; *The Sea* (Chichester Festival Theatre); *Celebration*;
Snogging Ken (Almeida Theatre) and *Far Away* (Royal
Court, Albery Theatre, West End).
Katherine recently formed theatre/film company
palimpsest.co

Alex McSweeney | Playwright / Director

His writing/directing credits include: his adaptation of Lermontov's *A Hero Of Our Time* (Rose Theatre Kingston/Zoo Edinburgh) and *Best Men/Between Women* (Hen and Chickens Theatre). His short plays have been performed at The Pleasance, London and The Tabernacle.

As an actor he has worked extensively across television, film and theatre, including recent work with Steven Berkoff including on *On The Waterfront* (Nottingham Playhouse and Theatre Royal Haymarket) and *Oedipus* (Liverpool Playhouse).

James Perkins | Designer

James has designed operas, musicals, classics and new writing for companies and venues both nationally and internationally.

Design credits include: *Little Shop of Horrors* (Royal Exchange Manchester); *Breeders* (St James Theatre); *Ciphers* (Out of Joint/Bush Theatre/UK tour); *Shiver*; *Lost In Yonkers* (Watford Palace Theatre); *Microcosm* (Soho Theatre); *Dances of Death* (Gate Theatre); *The Girl in The Yellow Dress* (Salisbury Playhouse); *Liar Liar*; *1001 Nights* (Unicorn Theatre); *The Fantasist's Waltz* (York Theatre Royal); *The Only True History of Lizzie Finn*; *Floyd Collins* (Southwark Playhouse); *The Hotel Plays* (site-specific at The Holborn Grand); *Matters of Life and Death* (UK tour); *Stockwell* (The Tricycle); *The Marriage of Figaro* (Wilton's Music Hall); *Life of Stuff*; *Desolate Heaven*; *Many Moons* (Theatre503); *St John's Night*; *Saraband* (Jermyn Street

Theatre); *Carthage*; *Foxfinder*; *Bofors Gun*; *Trying* (Finborough Theatre) *Orpheus and Troy Boy* (UK tour); *Iolanthe*; *The Way Through The Woods* (Pleasance London); *Pirates and Pinafore* (Buxton Opera House); *The Faerie Queen* (Lilian Baylis Studio) and *The Wonder* (BAC).

James created Story Whores. He is an associate of Forward Theatre Project and one third of paper/scissors/stone.

Gary Bowman | Lighting Designer

Gary trained at Bristol Old Vic Theatre School. Nominations include Best Lighting Designer for *Gotcha* in 2011 Off West End Awards. Gary was Deputy Chief Electrician at the Donmar Warehouse from 2009 to 2011.

Lighting design credits: *Titus Andronicus* (Theory of Everything/Bold Tendencies); *Holiday/The Eisteddfod* (Bussey Building); *The Act* (Trafalgar Studios 2); *Ciphers* (Out of Joint/Bush Theatre/UK tour); *Mana* (ACE Dance and Music/UK Tour); *Thark* (Park Theatre); *Even Stillness Breathes Softly Against A Brick Wall* (Soho Theatre); *Carthage*; *A Life*; *Foxfinder*; *Apart From George*; *S-27* (Finborough Theatre); *Liar Liar*; *1001 Nights* (Unicorn Theatre); *Feathers in the Snow*; *The Only True History of Lizzie Finn* (Southwark Playhouse); *Life for Beginners* (Theatre503); *Angle at the Bush* (Bush Theatre); *Gotcha*; *Mary Rose*; *Art of Concealment*; *Rubies in the Attic* (Riverside Studios); *Jest End* (Jermyn Street & Leicester Square Theatres) and *The Disappearance of Sadie Jones* (Bikeshed Exeter/UK Tour).

John Chambers | Composer / Sound Designer

John studied music composition at Trinity College of Music, where he was awarded the Daryl Runswick Composition Prize, the John Halford Composition Prize, and the Chappell Composition Prize.

Previous work includes: *Man to Man* (Park Theatre); *Macbeth* (Mercury Theatre Colchester); Steven Berkoff's *Oedipus* (Spoleto Festival USA, Edinburgh, Nottingham and Liverpool Playhouses); *Hey, Presto!*; *Bringing Down the Moon* (Peaceful Lion); *A Christmas Carol* (New Perspectives); *Biblical Tales* (New End Theatre) and *A Hero Of Our Time* (Rose Theatre Kingston, Edinburgh Festival). When he isn't working in theatre, John writes production music for use in TV and advertising, concert music, and fanfares for special occasions.

Simon Pittman | Movement Director

Simon is a theatre director and choreographer. He directs the multi-disciplinary company Rough Fiction, is a practitioner for Frantic Assembly, and has worked with a range of companies including The National Theatre of Scotland, The Library Theatre Manchester and Soho Theatre.

Recent work includes: movement and associate direction on *The Shawshank Redemption (*Edinburgh Festival / Gaiety Theatre, Dublin); *Ignition* (Frantic Assembly); *The Go-Between* (West Yorkshire Playhouse / Derby Live / Northampton) and direction on *The Last of The Lake* (Rough Fiction / UK Tour).

Jane Arnold-Forster | Production Manager
Previous productions include: *Thark* (Park Theatre); *Even Stillness Breathes Softly Against A Brick Wall* (Soho Theatre); *Ignorance* (Hampstead Theatre); *La Bohème*; *The Man on Her Mind* (Charing Cross Theatre); *A Life* (Finborough Theatre) and *The Only True History of Lizzie Finn* (Southwark Playhouse).
She was part of the production teams for *Port*; *The Captain of Kopenick* and *This House* at The Royal National Theatre.

Maeve Bolger | Company Stage Manager
Maeve is a graduate of RADA's Technical Theatre and Stage Management course.
Her theatre credits include *Enduring Song* – an original piece of writing by Jesse Briton performed at Southwark Playhouse and Jamie Wilkes' *The Bunker Trilogy* performed both at the Edinburgh Fringe Festival and the Seoul Performing Arts Festival in 2014.

Alicia Bloundele | Assistant Director
Director: *Alice by Heart* (Lyric Theatre, Hammersmith) and *Katherine - A Short Life* (Etcetera Theatre).
Assistant Director: *Multiplex* (The Olivier, Royal National Theatre); *White Feathers* (Rose Theatre Kingston) and *A Hero of our Time* (Rose Theatre Kingston).

Fine Line Productions | Producer
Fine Line Productions was founded by Lindsay Fraser in 2011.

Previous productions include: *When Did You Last See My Mother?* (Trafalgar Studios); *Execution Of Justice* (Southwark Playhouse) and *Even Stillness Breathes Softly Against A Brick Wall* (Soho Theatre).

Lindsay also runs the multi-award-winning theatre company Bear Trap where she produced *Bound* (Edinburgh Fringe, Adelaide Fringe, Southwark Playhouse, UK National Tour) which won a host of awards including a Fringe First; and *Enduring Song* (Southwark Playhouse).

Lindsay was the recipient of the Society of London Theatre's Stage One New Producers Bursary in October 2014.

Robyn Keynes | Associate Producer

Previous productions include: *East of Berlin* (Southwark Playhouse); *Velocity* (Finborough Theatre); *Catnip* (Arts Theatre); *A Modern Town* (Pleasance London and Edinburgh) and *Kitty Litter* (theSpaceUK, Edinburgh and The Courtyard, London).

As Assistant Producer: *Memphis* (Shaftesbury Theatre); *The Pajama Game* (Shaftesbury Theatre); *Boy In A Dress* (UK tour) and *The Bear*, a co-production with Improbable (UK tour).

Robyn was also Festival Co-ordinator of the National Student Drama Festival 2014.

Park Theatre is a theatre for London today. Our vision is to become a nationally and internationally recognised powerhouse of theatre.

★ ★ ★ ★ ★ *"A spanking new five-star neighbourhood theatre."* Independent

We opened in May 2013 and stand proudly at the heart of our diverse Finsbury Park community. With two theatres, a rehearsal and workshop space plus an all-day cafe bar, our mission is to be a welcoming and vibrant destination for all.

We choose plays based on how they make us feel: presenting classics through to new writing, musicals to experimental theatre all united by strong narrative drive and emotional content. In our first year we presented twenty-five plays including ten world premieres and two UK premieres, welcoming over a hundred and twenty seven thousand visitors through our doors.

Highlights included *Daytona*, with Maureen Lipman, which toured nationally and recently transferred to the West End, and *Yellow Face* which transferred to the National Theatre Shed.

"A first-rate new theatre in north London." Daily Telegraph

In our second year we're looking forward to growing our audience base, forging partnerships internationally and continuing to attract the best talent in the industry. Through a range of creative learning activities we're also working with all ages to nurture new audiences and develop the next generation of theatre practitioners.

To succeed in all of this ongoing support is of paramount importance. As a charity, with no public subsidy, none of this is possible without the help of our Friends, trusts and foundations and corporate sponsors. To find out more about us, our artistic programme and how you can support Park Theatre, please go to **parktheatre.co.uk**

OUT OF THE CAGE

by Alex McSweeney

In May 1915, Lloyd George was appointed Minister of Munitions, having engineered public outrage in the press concerning The Shell Crisis and Kitchener's part in it. The shortage of artillery shells for the heavy guns on the Western Front was dramatically compromising the British war effort. Lord Kitchener, Secretary of State for War, was accused in *The Times* and *The Mail* as being culpable for the "blunder". The ensuing political fall out left Lloyd George responsible for having to dramatically increase Britain's munitions output. The obvious problem was that there was a shortage of men to make the munitions. Britons had responded to Kitchener's rallying cry in their droves in the summer and autumn of 1914 (over a million had joined up). Where would the labour come from to make the weapons necessary for Britain's war effort? The problem was exacerbated when conscription was brought in in March 1916. The answer was the mobilization of Britain's women. And it is clear that women responded to this call. In August 1914, few women were working in munitions, in 1918, 950,000 were employed in the trade.

It is at this juncture that the horse-trading began. Lloyd George needed women, and he turned to Emmeline Pankhurst, leader of the Women's Social and Political Union, otherwise known as the Suffragettes (surprising as the Suffragettes had blown up his house in February 1913). Pankhurst, for her part, having suspended the campaign for female enfranchisement for the duration of the war, realized the advantages of proving that women could be as productive in Industry as men and the constant public viewing of women engaging in traditional male occupations as bus and taxi drivers, fire-wardens and policewomen would be, ultimately, beneficial to the cause of female equality. This relationship would, ultimately, be a contributing factor to women (over the age of 30) winning the right to vote in 1918. More problematic, however, was the response of men and, in particular, members of Trade Unions. The hard fought for rights that many Trade Unions had struggled for over the previous 50 years were jeopardized by the proposed 'dilution' of labour (the breaking down of complex activities and tasks into simplified activities that could be done by unskilled labour ie. women). Not wanting to risk a wave of strikes that would cripple Britain's war effort, Lloyd George agreed to the Trade Unions' demands that men returning from the war (and, in particular, the skilled workers) would be readmitted to their positions in the factories. But what would happen to the women who had been working so hard, and indeed dying, to produce the armaments to help bring about the proposed victory? Another concession to the Trade Unions was that women would continue to be paid less than men and that strict divisions of labour would continue to be enforced. It was these intractable positions that women had to fight against. Most women did leave industry, and particularly munitions, after the war but many did not go back to their pre-war jobs; 1.5 million did not return to domestic service (indeed, there was a servant crisis in middle and upper-class households after the war). They had been let **out of the cage** and many of them were determined not to go back in.

Dr. Alex McSweeney is a Senior Lecturer in English & Creative Writing at LSBU and a Lecturer in Drama at KU.

CHARACTERS

JANE BYASS: 40's, 4 kids, hard, fair, Sheffield.

NANCY LONGDON: Late 20's, upper-class, committed.

DEE JESSOP: 40's, dying, 7 kids, vengeful, London.

NELLY JONSON: 30's, forceful, sharp, Irish.

ANNIE CASTLEDINE: Early 20's, vibrant, funny, knowing, London.

CARRIE SEFTON: Early 20's, pretty, tough, engaging, London.

OL' MUM: 50's, nurturing, fair, evangelical, tough, London.

LIL' GINNY: Early teens, naïve, grafter, good girl, London

MRS. BILLINGS (offstage only – doubles with **OL' MUM**): Landlady, London.

WOMEN WORKERS *enter, exhausted, upstage. End of shift. They begin to brush off the dirt, wipe off the grease, and change out of their overalls. Singing:*

Not the Girls You Left Behind You

> *We're not your angels in the aisles*
> *Not your lovelies in the streets......*

Lights up on Scene: a bedsit. London. Worn but clean. Spring 1916.

JANE BYASS *enters, a package under her arm. Urgent. Followed by* **LIL' GINNY** *carrying two bags. She stands with the bags in her hand.* **JANE** *walks over to a small table at the side of the room and turns a table lamp on.*

JANE:	(*Taking her hat off*) Pop 'em on, Gin.
LIL' GINNY:	Miss. Byass?
JANE:	Pop 'em on, girl. Pop 'em on. Else they'll drop off.
LIL' GINNY:	Pop 'em on?
JANE:	The table, Ginny. The table. You'll not turn to stone. The bags.
LIL' GINNY:	(*Moving to the table*) Right you are, Miss. Byass.
JANE:	Good girl. (*Rummaging in her pocket. Palming a coin*) That's yours.
LIL' GINNY:	No, no, no, Miss Byass. Not a song...

JANE:	Workers in the dusk, Ginny Mae.
LIL' GINNY:	Not me, Miss Byass.
JANE:	It'll hit the pot.
LIL' GINNY:	No, no… I know my way, Miss Byass.
JANE:	You're a good girl, Ginny. On your way. And slip out.
LIL' GINNY:	I's 'opin'….
JANE:	On your way, girl. An' keep it to yours.
LIL' GINNY:	But…
JANE:	But never you mind. Slip down and pull that door easy on the road.
LIL' GINNY:	But Miss Byass…
JANE:	There's no 'buts' now. Push on, Ginny.
LIL' GINNY:	I's 'ere 'cos I want to…
JANE:	There's no time for buts now. (*Edging her out*) Ease the door.
LIL' GINNY:	Miss Byass…
JANE:	This ain't for you, Ginny. On your way.

Voices can be heard downstairs and moments later there is a soft knock at the door. **JANE** *walks over to the door and opens it.* **NANCY LONGDON** *stands in the doorway. She is tall and*

immaculately dressed. She looks past **JANE** *and* **LIL' GINNY**
(lingering) and surveys the room.

JANE: (*Gesturing into the room*) Come in.

NANCY: (*Entering*) Is there no one here?

JANE: Not yet.

NANCY: Am I early?

JANE: Erm... No, I don't think so. Everybody's late, I think. (*To* **LIL' GINNY**) Thank you, Ginny. (*Firm*) Good of you.

LIL' GINNY: Yes.

NANCY: Hello, Ginny.

LIL' GINNY: Ma'am.

JANE: Off you go, Gin. An' thanks. Easy as you go.

NANCY: Goodbye, Ginny.

LIL GINNY: Ma'am.

JANE: Good girl.

LIL' GINNY: I'll....

JANE: That's it, girl.

LIL' GINNY *exits.*

NANCY *looks around the room being sure to avoid displaying any disdain or disapproval at her surroundings.*

JANE:	Did Mrs. Billings let you in? Sit down, if you like.
NANCY:	Thank you. (*Briefly looking down at the chair before sitting*). I believe so, yes. Seems pleasant enough.
JANE:	Yes, she is. She's going to bring up some hot water for us. For the tea. I can't offer you anything 'til then. Mrs. Billings doesn't allow anything stronger in the house. That's one of her golden's with us.
NANCY:	Quite. Probably not a bad thing.

Beat.

JANE:	It's... good of you to come.
NANCY:	Not at all. (*Beat*) Are we expecting many?
JANE:	I think so. I hope so. I think everybody's running late.
NANCY:	They're not at the beck and call of the maroon here.
JANE:	Yes, that's probably it.

(Awkward) silence.

JANE:	Have you had to come far?
NANCY:	Not so very far.
JANE:	That's good. (*Beat*) By tram?

NANCY:	Yes.
JANE:	More reliable.
NANCY:	Quite.-
JANE:	So, where is it that you... reside?
NANCY:	Curzon Street. Not so very far.
JANE:	Very nice.
NANCY:	Yes, I suppose it is. (*Beat*) It's my aunt's house. It's convenient. For the effort.
JANE:	Of course. Not from London?
NANCY:	No, Hampshire.
JANE:	Lovely.
NANCY:	Yes. It can be. (*Looking around*) This is nice. Adequate for the purpose, I mean.
JANE:	I'm happy. Could be worse. From what I've seen of other places. Some of the girls, I mean... doesn't bear thinking about. Some of the places...
NANCY:	So, I've heard.
JANE:	Mrs. Billings is a bit... she likes things her way.
NANCY:	I'm sure.

JANE:	She's been fair with me since I've been here. She's allowed the young 'uns to visit, once in a while.
NANCY:	That's good of her.
JANE:	She's had a bit of trouble. With some of the girls. In the past.
NANCY:	I'm sure she has.
JANE:	Can't hold it against them, I suppose. They're not used to it all. The freedom.
NANCY:	Let's hope we get something done tonight.
JANE:	I've got everything prepared. I think we just need to discuss a few things.
NANCY:	Yes. Ways to move forward.
JANE:	That's it. The way forward. (*Beat*) It's important for the girls, all of us, that some of you are with us.
NANCY:	Why wouldn't *we* be with you?
JANE:	Well... it's just important that we...
NANCY:	Speak as one.
JANE:	That's it. A united front.
NANCY:	I can assure you that it's what we all want.
JANE:	Well, it means a lot. That's all I'm saying. To the girls.

NANCY: Quite.

Beat.

NANCY: What's on the agenda? For the evening?

JANE: Minutes. Then suggestion for progress and parity.

NANCY: Minutes?

JANE: Of the last meeting.

NANCY: You've met before…?

Voices can be heard downstairs again.

JANE: (*Listening*) Oh, this sounds like someone…

JANE *looks expectantly at the door. Moments later, there is a timid knock on the door.* **JANE** *crosses to the door and opens it.* **DEE JESSOP** *stands in the doorway. She is a slight woman in her forties. Her skin has a yellow hue that accentuates her sunken features. Her eyes are slightly red and swollen. The hair at the front of her head, protruding from her hat, is an orangey yellow. She is out of breath.*

DEE *enters the room.* **NANCY** *rises from her chair.*

NANCY: Hello, Dee. Would you like to sit down?

DEE *waves away the suggestion. She tries to catch her breath but begins coughing. Her cough is a deep, raking one.* **NANCY** *and* **JANE** *look at each other with concern.* **DEE** *finally catches her breath.*

29

DEE:	I'm all right. I'm all right. Don't you worry about me. I'm all right. Jus' catchin' me breath.
JANE:	There's some tea on its way, Dee.
DEE:	That'll be nice. A nice cuppa.
NANCY:	Are you sure you won't sit down, Dee? Just for a moment?
DEE:	No, ma'am (*Looking to* **JANE**) er... Miss Longdon... er...
NANCY:	Nancy.
DEE:	Nancy. Yes, Nancy. Thank you, ma'am.
Beat.	
NANCY:	Dee, have you been to see the doctor?
DEE:	I'm all right. I'm all right.
NANCY:	But have you been examined recently?
JANE:	Won't do any good. Livsey looks inside your mouth and passes you.
NANCY:	Well, we'll have to do something. I'll talk to Mr. Collins.
JANE:	Won't do any good.
NANCY:	She must be pulled out of C. E. work, at the very least.

DEE: I'm all right. I just gets a little out of breath.

JANE: Dee, your eyes are puffing out your sockets. (*Examining* **DEE**'s *hands*) Look at her hands. Look at the swelling.

NANCY: You need some rest, Dee.

JANE: She needs a clearing sheet and there's an end on it.

DEE: I don't need no clearing sheet. I don't want no clearing sheet. I'm all right.

JANE: As long as someone doesn't light a match near you or you drop down dead.

DEE: I jus' gets a little out of breath, thass all. An' me mouf a little bit.

JANE: Let's have a look. (*Looking into* **DEE**'s *mouth*). (*To* **NANCY**) Have you seen this?

NANCY *walks over and looks into* **DEE**'s *mouth.*

NANCY: When were you last examined, Dee?

DEE: When was it? Wednesday week, think it was.

NANCY: Dr. Livsey examined you last week and passed you?

DEE: That's right. A week Wednesday, it was.

NANCY:	You're sure of that, Dee?
DEE:	Sure as I'm standing 'ere.
NANCY:	Did he say anything to you?
DEE:	'E asked me if I'd been on the burst?
JANE:	Hah!
DEE:	I told 'im if he never drank more than me he'd not go far wrong. I also told 'im I'd sons fighting for the likes of him.
JANE:	(*To* **NANCY**) D'you see? This is what we're saying. This is what we're doing.
NANCY:	Yes, I see. I see. (To **DEE**) Dee, I'm going to talk to Mr. Collins.
DEE:	No need for that. I don't want no fuss. No, no.
NANCY:	I'm just …
DEE:	No, no. I'm all right. Don't worry 'bout me.
JANE:	Dee, we'll just get you out of cordite for a bit. 'Till you get your breath.
DEE:	No, no. Don't you do that. I'm all right. Don't you do that. That's my rate. That's the rate I need.
NANCY:	But Dee….
DEE:	Don't do nothin'. That's my rate.

JANE: All right, Dee. We just trying to help. That's why...

DEE: That's my rate. I'm just down 'ere for my bit. Just doin' what's right, thass all but I don't want no fuss.

JANE: All right, Dee. No fuss.

Silence.

JANE: People will be here soon. I don't think we should start until some others are here.

NANCY: I don't think there'd be much point.

JANE: Shouldn't be too long.

Voices can be heard downstairs. A loud distinctive voice stands out. **JANE** *moves over to the door and listens.*

JANE: This'll be Nelly.

JANE *stands expectantly by the door. After a moment there is a decisive knock at the door.* **JANE** *opens it.* **NELLY JOHNSON** *pauses momentarily at the door before entering. She is a sharp-featured, dark-haired woman in her late twenties.*

NELLY: How's the one downstairs?

JANE: Mrs. Billings? She's all right.

NELLY: Mrs. Billings, is it?

JANE: She's fine.

NELLY: Is she?

JANE: Yes, she's fine.

NELLY *turns to see* **NANCY.**

NELLY: What's she doing here?

JANE: She's here for the meeting.

NELLY: I'll bet.

JANE: She wanted to come.

NELLY: Of course she did.

NANCY: It's all right, Jane. I can speak for myself.

NELLY: Of course you can. With all that wonderful instruction you've had; you can speak for all of us. And eloquently, at that.

NANCY: I've as much right to be here as anyone else.

NELLY: Sure you have. All that hard grafting you've been doing. Three years or the duration, is it? I'm sure.

NANCY: I want what's best for all the girls.

NELLY: 'Course you do. 'Till you go home to your china tea set and comfortable, aired bed. And don't expect thanks from them girls.

NANCY: I don't.

NELLY: Good. 'Cos most of 'em go home to eight in a room and a bed the day-worker just left.

JANE:	Why don't we come to an understanding that we're trying to work together. For the common good.
NANCY:	Quite.
NELLY:	Who's common good are we talking about?
JANE:	I think its best if we try and...
NELLY:	Well, if there's a tip off at least we'll know where it came from.
NANCY:	That's ridiculous! The idea that I would...
JANE:	Please. Please, we must work together. Nelly, please!
NELLY:	We'll see.
JANE:	Nelly!
NELLY:	Mark my words.
DEE:	If it's goin' to be shoutin' all night, I'll be off. That's all I know.

DEE *descends into another coughing fit. The other three women look on helplessly.* **NELLY** *walks over to assist her but* **DEE** *waves her away.*

NELLY:	Dee, sit down a moment.
DEE:	(*Catching her breath*) I don't want no fuss. I'm all right. I'm here to do my bit an see

whats wot but if there's goin' to be shoutin' an that, I'm back on the tram home.

JANE: Don't worry Dee. There won't be any shouting.

NANCY: Of course not, Dee.

NELLY: (*Gesturing towards* **DEE**) Look at her! And that's acceptable to the management?! That's for the war effort?! Look at her. It won't be long now. Mark my words.

Beat.

NANCY: Look, do you think we should start?

JANE: Should we?

NANCY: Are there others expected?

NELLY: Would you like us to jot the names down to save you waiting?

JANE: I'm sure there'll be more. I suppose we could start by having a read. (*Going to a cupboard,* **JANE** *pulls out a handful of newspapers*). Here we are. I don't know if anybody's read the latest edition. I brought them in case anybody was interested.

JANE *hands out a newspaper to each of the women.* **NANCY** *takes her copy, briefly glances at it and then folds it up and places it on her coat.* **DEE** *stares at the cover blankly.*

NELLY: (*Reading*) "*Woman Worker*"... '*The Home Secretary's recent announcement that qualified women will be licensed to drive public vehicles in London has resulted in large numbers applying for posts as taxi-drivers. At 2 schools of motoring altogether about 100 women are now studying the 'knowledge of London' test, which has to be passed before Scotland Yard grants a licence.* Lucky us! Let's have a National Holiday! (*Reading on*) *Meanwhile men members of the London and Provincial Union of Licensed Vehicle Workers are taking a ballot on the proposal to cease work directly the first woman appears in London as a driver of a licensed vehicle. The result of this step remains to be seen.* (*To* **JANE**) I don't know why you bother reading this. You play straight into their hands.

NANCY: Whose hands are "they"?

NELLY: Why, the ruling elite, Ms Longdon. All your lot. Divide and rule. (*Curtsying*) (If that will be all, ma'am? I shall retire downstairs to scramble for the pittance you allow the working class to fight each other for every day).

JANE: Look, Nelly. We're all here to try and cover common ground and consolidate our position and I think Nancy is here for the same.

NANCY: I'm here to help as best I can.

NELLY: Well, that's very kind of you. (Very kind of you indeed). It must be unfortunate to have to descend into such depravity and frightfulness.

JANE: Nelly, Please. We need to be civil.

NELLY: (*To* **JANE**) Do you have any more literature. Some pamphets, perhaps? (*To* **NANCY**). What about you? Any NUWSS pamphlets about your person?

NANCY: I'm sorry to disappoint you.

NELLY: But you are a member?

NANCY: Thank you for your concern but I am not.

NELLY: Not a member of so benevolent a society?

NANCY: I have certain sympathies with their cause but I am not a member.

NELLY: I suppose it is rather unladylike.

JANE: I suppose we should begin. What do you think? Shall we vote on it?

DEE: What? The four of us 'ere? Doesn't seem worth it. Let's just get on with it.

JANE: Are we all agreed? (*Beat*) The first concern to bring to the management's attention, I think, is…

As **JANE** *searches for her notes under a pile of papers on the dresser, the sound of singing can be heard coming from downstairs followed by voices and some laughter. The four women exchange glances.* **NELLY** *makes her way over to the door and listens. She is followed by* **JANE**. *The voices and laughter become louder. Eventually the singing comes to a halt. Muffled laughter can be heard from behind the door. The singing begins again.*

Wouldn't he look handsomer in khaki?

Wouldn't he look fine in uniform?

Wouldn't it make your life worthwhile, to see his handsome smile

As he marches off and soldiers up a storm

JANE *opens the door. In the doorway stands* **ANNIE CASTLEDINE**, *a good-looking, vivacious woman in her early twenties. And* **CARRIE SEFTON** *(who stops singing as soon as the door opens), a pretty girl of about twenty.*

JANE: (*Holding her finger to her lips. Desperately*) Ssshhhhh!

ANNIE *and* **CARRIE** *look at* **JANE** *and then over to an unimpressed* **NELLY** *scowling at them with her arms crossed. Beat. They burst into laughter. After a moment.*

ANNIE:	(*Entering*) Evenin' all. Not too late, are we? (*Beat*) (*To* **CARRIE**) Do it again, Carrie. Please. I love it so.
CARRIE:	(*Singing*)

Wouldn't he look handsomer in khaki?

Wouldn't he look fine in uniform?

ANNIE joins in (*her voice is not as good*).

CARRIE	*Wouldn't it make your life worthwhile,*
ANNIE:	*To see his handsome smile…*
JANE:	Ssshhhh! Pipe down, you two. You'll have us all thrown out.
NELLY:	Have you two been drinking?
ANNIE:	Drinking? (*To* **CARRIE**) Have we been drinking, Carrie?
CARRIE:	Us? Drinking? I've never 'eard the like!
ANNIE:	The cheek of it! Accusin' us. Of drinkin'!!?? (*Noticing* **NANCY**) Blow me down if it ain't the Duchess of Pimlico. Look Carrie, it's old Lady Whatnot.
CARRIE:	(*Curtsies mockingly*) 'Ow do yer?
ANNIE:	Where's the other two?
NANCY:	I'm not sure to whom you're referring.

ANNIE: You know, Lady Meeow an' her chum.

NANCY: If you're referring to Miss Bingham and Miss Clarendon, they shan't be joining us.

ANNIE: That don't surprise me, m'lady. (*To* **CARRIE**) They are otherwise engaged, Miss Sefton.

CARRIE: 'Ow do 'ave us, Miss Castledine.

NELLY: If you two are going…

MRS. BILLINGS V. O.:   Everything all right in their Ms. Byass?

JANE: (*Through the door*) Yes, thank you, Mrs. Billings.

V. O.:   Could I have a quick word, please?

JANE: Now?

V. O.:   Yes, thank you.

JANE looks over at ANNIE and CARRIE. She opens the door and slips out the door. Beat. A heated discussion takes place a little way from the door concerning drinking and singing etc. The occupants of the room stand in silence listening. ANNIE and CARRIE try not to look at each other for fear of laughing. After a time the door opens and JANE re-enters. Beat. ANNIE and CARRIE burst into barely stifled laughter.

JANE: Right. If you two have any alcohol, I want you to give it over.

41

ANNIE: (*Singing*)

Think of your heart swelling when you see him,

CARRIE: (*Joining in*)

Standing there with medals on his chest.

JANE: (*Firmly*) Annie?

ANNIE: We 'aven't got any. We met some of them proper smart kiddies up the hill and they bought us a couple o 'alf n blacks, thass all.

CARRIE: 'Ow do yer! Weren't they smashing, Annie?

ANNIE: Weren't they juss. And weren't one of them makin' the glad eye at you.

CARRIE: *Wouldn't he look fine in uniform?*

DEE: (*Getting up*) Are we startin' this or I'll be off 'ome.

ANNIE: Blow me down. Don't no one strike a match, we'll all go up. 'Ow are yer, Dee?

DEE: Better for seein' you. I'm doin' my bit.

ANNIE: An' good for you, too.

CARRIE: Blimey, you look like you've gone off, Dee Jessop. Look, she looks worse than those Jones girls.

NELLY: And if we're not careful that's what we all end up looking like so let's begin.

A spotlight snaps up on **CARRIE**

CARRIE:

> Keep that lathe turnin'
> Clear the screw-threads
> Gauge the banger depth
> Paint them monsters, row on row
> An' keep that devil's porridge off yer skin
> We all lose our looks 'ere
> They said it first an' they said it straight
> You come in sweet an' soft
> And leave with a face past prayin' for
> Like the paint on them dump shells
> We go out as yellow as custard tart
> Strike a match an' we're all gone
> Reenie Smith got three months 'cos a match
> Got caught in the lining of her pocket
> An' come out flying when she pulled 'er 'anky out
> We all lose our looks here
> Thass your medal on your chest.

Spotlight snaps down.

JANE: Right. I'll see if I can get Mrs. Billings to hurry up with that hot water.

NELLY: Fuck the tea. We'll have it after.

JANE: Right. (*Going to the cupboard*) We've made a list of proposals and grievances (*Taking out a writing book*). I think this could be the basis for our meeting with the management.

NELLY: There's no point having a meeting with them.

JANE: We need to sit down with them and discuss the way to move forward.

NELLY: Waste of time.

NANCY: Well, clearly, we have to let them know about our unhappiness with certain aspects...

NELLY: It won't do any good. They know all about our "unhappiness with certain aspects". There's only one thing they understand. Force. We've got to shut the whole place down. Bring the whole place to a standstill. Halt the means of production. And then they'll listen.

Silence.

NANCY: Are you suggesting a strike?

NELLY: Yes. Shut everything down and stand by our machines. Sabotage them if necessary. Bring them to their knees.

NANCY:	They'll just bring more men in.
NELLY:	They're with us.
JANE:	Are they? Which ones?
NELLY:	The setters-up, the mechanics, they're all with us. They know there's only one way to stop this slaughter.
JANE:	I'm not sure…
NANCY:	I'm not sure you'll find much support for those views.
NELLY:	'Course we won't from you.
NANCY:	From anyone.
NELLY:	One day, we'll reach up and pull you down. All of you. Parasites.
JANE:	I think our demands…
NELLY:	No demands.
JANE:	But we've made an…
NELLY:	No demands. Stop the war. Stop the slaughter. Stop the lies. No shells, no war. No bullets, no war. Unity with our fellow workers in Germany, France, everywhere. All out strike and no more shells made. Bring the slaughterers to their knees.

Silence.

DEE:	Just my rate. What's due 'n' fair. Thass all. Just what's fair.
NELLY:	They don't care about fair. Fair doesn't come into it. We're fodder for the machine. All of us. The capitalist machine.
DEE:	Don't know 'bout all that. Fair rate for fair work. All equals, like.
ANNIE:	You tell 'er, Dee. She'll 'ave you up the junction no time, duck.
NELLY:	Never you mind, Annie Castledine, they'll spit you out any time soon.
ANNIE:	Don't you worry 'bout Annie Castledine. She takes it as it comes. Don't you worry 'bout her.
NELLY:	For how long?
ANNIE:	You go on, Missus Cluck.
NELLY:	All cosy, sure you are now. They need you now. And happy you are in your sets 'n' shingles. But you're surplus. Like all of us. And where are you after? When the men come home.
CARRIE:	Don't care if they do, if you ask me. My ole man, 'ope he don't. (*Beat*) And there it is. Tin of evil, as 'e is. No place on this earth for 'im. 'Ope 'e cops it over there.

DEE:	Carrie Sefton, you set that tongue of yours.
CARRIE:	Don't care who knows it. Don't care who knows it. Don't care who knows. Send 'em round 'n' I'll tell it to their face. I 'ope he cops it over there. Evil bastard. From birth. An'll die the same. An' won't I dance a merry one, an all.
DEE:	You leave all that to yourself an' yours. Don't you do that here. Not here, Carrie Sefton. With all your spark 'n' shine.
CARRIE:	An' 'ere's you. Ain't that fine? Dee Jessop with all 'ers. Thass a joke on high. Kissin' the shells an' high. Every one. Gives it a special send off, her. Don't you Dee? Special send off for all o' them. Kiss of death, every one. You 'n' your specials. Here's for you, Fritz. A special good 'un. Hope it takes you all out an you drown in your own blood...
JANE:	All right, Carrie...
CARRIE:	No, no, she'll have 'em all swimming in blood. Won't bring 'im back, Dee.
DEE:	You leave off that tongue, Carrie Sefton.
CARRIE:	It won't. 'E's gone an thass that. 'An 'es done 'is. 'An 'e did it good, Dee. But 'e ain't comin' back...

47

JANE: Carrie…

DEE: You cut that tongue of yours, Carrie Sefton or I'll cut it for you…

CARRIE: Wouldn't make it, Dee. You'll puff out 'alf over here. You got a pant 'n' beat in you and thass that. You'll keel over on the way. 'E ain't comin' back, Dee. I'm sorry for you 'n' yours. 'E was a good 'un, all accounts but we're us. Thass all we got. Us. We've got to keep on. They'll skin us if we don't. Don't hold no candle. Its us 'n' them at the end of it. With some of them. Ain't it so, Annie.

ANNIE: *Wouldn't it make your life worthwhile.*

A low hum begins.

JANE: Ladies, please. I really think we should be getting on.

NANCY: Here, here.

CARRIE: Cluck, cluck.

JANE: I think we should start. Decisions need to be made. We need to come to some agreement. For the other sections.

NELLY: All out, that's what we tell 'em.

NANCY: Mrs. Johnson, we are here to ensure better treatment for the girls…

NELLY: And a lot of good it will do.

A spotlight snaps up on **NANCY**

NANCY:

> I'll not deny it, when I first walked in
> Through those enormous iron gates
> I thought they were all vulgar little hussies
> Rough, shrill, over-bearing vulgar hussies.
> All shabbily dressed but with aims at finery
> Carried out in a cheap and tawdry manner.
> But it was the men,
> The men that were the real problem.
> Little cared they for the war effort
> The foreman, like many of them, had refused to enlist
> The insolence,
> Insolence from a class of men that I had
> Always been treated with deference was frightful.

Spotlight snaps down

JANE:	(*Opening her note book*) I've made a list of grievances and proposals.
NANCY:	I think the least we could do is listen to them.
DEE:	'Else I'm off on the tram.
CARRIE:	After you, Miss Byass. You take the reins.

JANE:	Thank you. This is an initial list of demands which are not negotiable: (*Reading*)
	1. Greater screening by doctor for yellowing and TNT poisoning, mouth ulcers and other symptoms.
	2. Worker's crèche.
	3. An end to Clearing Sheets.
	4. An investigation into hostels for workers.
	5. Opening up to women workers of skilled labour positions.
NANCY:	I really think we should be concentrating on rather more important things. Equal pay with the men. We do the same work. We must demand the same pay.
JANE:	I'm coming to that, Nancy.
ANNIE:	Hark at *Nancy*!
JANE:	(*To* **NELLIE**) You say the men are with us. But which ones? Bob Tell and his – not wanting to be undercut by us or Leather Frank Myers lot who don't want us getting the same as them?
ANNIE:	Shirkers, the lot of them!
JANE:	Annie!
ANNIE:	Every one of them!

NELLY: Annie Castledine, don't you go slipping.

ANNIE: Every one. Shame on them. Lurking around here. Sauntering about. Skulking in the shadows. Shame on them. All kushi. They know where they ought to be an' it ain't here. All nice 'n' cosy, whilst there's others doin' their work. The work that's got to be done. Else we'll all cop it. My Billy went straight off. First in line 'e was. Answered the call. Doin' 'is bit. Leather Frank and Bob Tell?! Don't make me laugh. Billy Noble's your man. Your *man*. Noble by name and nature. So, I carry my feathers just for them.

JANE: Annie!

ANNIE: That's right. Always carry my feathers. Everywhere I go. I'll pin 'ole the lot of them. Every one that's skulking in the shadows. All of 'em that I see gets one of Annie's feathers. One of Annie's sweet white feathers.

JANE: Annie, I don't think this is the time for...

NELLY: And where do you think they come from? These feathers? These white feathers you're popping on everyone's chest?

ANNIE: Don't care where they come from as long as they go to the right place.

NELLY: All them boys. Sending them to hell. Piercing their skin with those feathers of yours. Those poor boys.

ANNIE: Windy boys living the life.

CARRIE: I'm out of this one.

NELLY: Those poor boys. Skittled out before they've grown. Not even men. Not a chance. An' she's feathering them. Handing them out like hats on Derby Day. Shame on *you*. Where'd you think these feathers come from? Falling out the sky like manna from heaven? All these feathers from knowhere. You're a fool, Annie Castledine. And worse than that, you're a monkey. A monkey on their machine. Pay you a penny and you start moving. And handing them out for who? The Old Welsh goat's got you. You're doing his job twice. King and Country. Empire days. Them feathers coming out of his factories sure as them shells. Part of the war effort.

DEE: They're from birds, ain't they?

NELLY: Cough your guts up if they are, Dee Jessop!

JANE: What are you saying, Nelly?

NELLY: Come on. Don't tell me you don't know.

Reciting from memory.

"To the Women of Britain
Some of your men folk are holding back
On your account."

"Won't you prove your love for your
country
By persuading them to go?"

ANNIE: (*Singing over* **NELLY**)

Wouldn't he look handsomer in khaki?
Wouldn't he look fine in uniform?
Wouldn't it make your life worthwhile, to see
his handsome smile
As he marches off and soldiers up a storm.

NELLY: "To the women of Britain
When the war is over and
And someone asks your husband
Or your son what he did in the Great War,
Is he to hang his head because you would
not let him go."

ANNIE: They all go down my way, don't you worry.

NELLY: Sure they do. Straight into the ground.

JANE: I think we should move on....

The hum has got louder.

NELLY: You sleep tight, Annie Castledine. You
sleep tight, sending them boys off. Let's
wait till you get the letter. Let's see when

53

your Billy's in the ground. Blown half ways to Timbuctoo.

CARRIE: That's it, bogger! Don't tip it.

ANNIE: You keep going, Nelly Johnson an' we'll see.

NELLY: In the ground.

ANNIE: Don't worry 'bout my Billy.

NANCY: I really think that's quite enough!

NELLY: Sure, they don't send you a thing. Do you know that? (*Indicating* **NANCY**) Her lot does. They get something back. Don't you, m'lady. They get some effects, a watch, notebook, a hat, something, all caked, all stinking. But you? You get a letter. "I regret to inform you... death was instantaneous and no suffering was..."

ANNIE *rushes towards* **NELLY. CARRIE, NANCY** *and* **JANE** *jump towards* **ANNIE** *to stop her.*

ANNIE: I'll cut that tongue of yours...

CARRIE: Ssshhh! Listen! All of you! Listen! LISTEN! It's one of 'em.

CARRIE *rushes to the window. She pulls one of the curtains slightly too.*

JANE: Don't twitch it.

54

CARRIE: It's one of 'em.

NANCY: Carrie, you shouldn't...

CARRIE: Carrie do, Carrie don't. Never you mind.

JANE: You close that curtain.

CARRIE: It's one of'em, I'm telling you. Listen!

The women listen in Silence.

NANCY: Turn out the light! Immediately.

CARRIE: Listen!

Deep blue light. Silence. All the women stand motionless. The hum, a monotonous drone, has becoming increasingly deafening. JANE goes to the light and extinguishes it. The women stand in darkness for some time and listen.

DEE: I'm off 'ome.

CARRIE: Don't move, Dee. You'll go up.

NANCY: Best to stay inside, they say, Dee.

JANE: SSSSSHHHHH, LISTEN.

The drone has reached it peak. The women are frozen.

JANE: It's overhead.

They all look up. They all listen in silence as the drone moves away and the noise begins to subside.

DEE: (*Making to go*) That's me.

JANE: We haven't started yet.

DEE: That's me. (*Pointing upwards*) If *they're* about, that's me.

JANE: Let's just go through some of our demands.

DEE: I don't care about no demands with them things about.

NANCY: Dee, the safest place is here.

DEE: (*Beginning to panic*) Those things. Those 'orrible things. Above us. 'Ow they getting all the way over here? 'Ow they getting through? He was right. He was bleedin' right about the lot of 'em. 'Ow they getting' all the way over here. He was right, my 'ole man. The 'ole problem is all the royal family is bloody Germans. The Georges, they was all bloody German. Now take Queen Vic, she was a bloody German. King Edward, 'e was a bloody German. An' King George, 'e's a bloody German, so it stands to reason. Stands to bloody reason.

NANCY: Dee, pull yourself together.

JANE: Dee, come and sit down.

DEE: ALL BLOODY GERMANS!

CARRIE: (*Laughing*) That's the girl, Dee.

NELLY: Penny's dropped in Dee Jessop's corner.

DEE:	ALL BLOODY GERMANS. THE LOT OF THEM!
NANCY:	Dee, there's no need for that sort of thing.
NELLY:	(*Mimicking*) No need for that sort of frightfulness here, Dee.
JANE:	Nelly, don't...
NANCY:	I think we've all had enough of your... Bolshevist leanings for one day.
NELLY:	Bolshevist, is it? Bolshevist, she says.
ANNIE:	She's saying, where d'you park your bike at night? Ain't that right Duchess?
NELLY:	What d'you mean?
ANNIE:	There's turf in your fire.
NELLY:	Meaning what?
ANNIE:	Trot your bog. The lot of you.
NELLY:	Oh, that's it, is it?
ANNIE:	We know what side you lot are on.
NELLY:	The only sides are us and them. Proletariat and parasites.
ANNIE:	Paddy's with the Kaiser, that's what my Billy says.
NELLY:	I'm not *with* anyone.

ANNIE: You know it, doncha Duchess?

NELLY: I'm no West Brit neither.

NANCY: There's no call for unpatriotic behaviour. Not now. We are here to come to some common agreement as to how we move forward. With the management. We have to be organised for them to take us seriously. We wear a badge, ladies. It is a badge of honour and regarded as so. "On War Service". We're as much a part of this war as any man and should be respected as so. And we deserve to be remunerated equally as the men.

CARRIE: Wot's she on about?

ANNIE: Paid, duck. Remunerated means paid.

CARRIE: Thass all we want. Equals.

NANCY: And that's what we shall achieve, Carrie. The girls are paid 2s. 6d for a morning shift – the men get 3s. 9d. The girls get 2s. 9d for an afternoon shift – the men 4s. 2d. For the night shift, the girls are getting 3s. 3d – the men 4s. 6d.

NELLY: The *girls*, is it? Are you not taking a wage yourself?

NANCY: The girls. We. Myself. We deserve equal pay with the men.

ANNIE: You tell 'em, duchess.

CARRIE: But we don't do the same job.

JANE: What?

CARRIE: Well, we don't, do we? The setters-up, the mechanics, the foremen... they all do their own things...

JANE: Do you not think we could do all those things, Carrie?

ANNIE: 'Course we could. We ain't even allowed to sharpen our own tools. Waiting for your machine to be set up – you ask the wrong bloke an 'e tells you "do it yourself. We ain't allowed, I says. Well don't expect me to do it – I'm an operator! Well, lardy da, I says. Get me a setter up then. Get 'im yourself!" Them shirkers hate us being there 'cos they're ashamed of themselves.

JANE: It's not that, Annie. A mechanic can't set up a machine – that's the setter ups jobs. And a setter up can't operate a machine – that's the operator's job. The foremen can't touch the machines either. It's the trades unions. They look after their own and we've got to look after ourselves.

NELLY: They're not looking after themselves. They're looking after the workers against capitalist exploitation.

59

ANNIE:	Paddywack, paddywack.
NELLY:	I've a brother swimming in it as well, you know. Filling his lungs with poison over there. D'yer think its just your Billy an' his like slipping under? An' I'm telling you they're ready. For it all to come down.
JANE:	This is what I'm saying. This is why we're here. We've got to stick together. The men hate the idea of us undercutting them. Their rate. So they'll fight to keep us from the skilled jobs. But they also hate the idea of us earning as much as them. Three strikes they've voted for in the year I've been here and not once have we been included or even notified. Yes, there's common ground – an end to peace rates and clearing sheets but we've got to look after ourselves. Dolly Wright's family got nothing, not a penny. Fourteen months she did here and she's out in a wooden box without so much as a fare thee well. Them kiddies of hers got nothing. How many's that since Christmas last? Reenie Day, Kerry Foster, those other two and the Jones' girls. And Livsey passes them soon as you like. We want insurance medical and our dependents taken care of in the event. And an end to loitering fines and the like. We want respect. We deserve respect. We

deserve equal pay. Don't tell me we can't take down those machines, strip them down. Don't tell me we can't maintain the gauge tables, do the running repairs, handle the turn keys and the lever gauges. I've raised four kids with me bare hands with help from no man I've ever met. I've kept a house together on 3s. 6d. a week, one meal a day and scrapping for bread. I've sewn till me fingers bled. I've washed that many shirts for people as I thought me back would never straighten. I've walked ten miles with the soles out of my shoes for work an' I don't intend to do it again. So, don't tell me I can't maintain me own lathe and operate a lever without some man hanging over my shoulder. And don't tell me I'm not worth the money same as them. 'Cos I'm not going back. I'm here now and I'm not going back. So who's with me?

ANNIE: All the way, Jane, my girl. All the way!

CARRIE: I'll have some of that.

NANCY: What's to be done? That's the decision we need to…

NELLY: We've got to bring them to their knees…

ANNIE: We're not havin' none of that revolution in the streets malarkey.

NELLY: It's the only way…

NANCY: What is realistic in terms our demands.

JANE: Strike.

Beat.

CARRIE: A strike?

DEE: (*Rather faint*) Ooooohhh.

CARRIE: You sit down a mo', Dee.

ANNIE: Push on, Janey girl.

JANE: Get the support of those on our section and get them to come out with us. Strike.

DEE: Strike?

JANE: Get all the women out with us. All together. As one. All out. Strike.

ANNIE: Strike.

JANE: One chance. For our voices to be heard. Here and now. Strike.

NANCY: Strike.

JANE: Never go back. Unite, fight… and strike.

All the women look at each other… uncertain…

NELLY: Jesus wept! Strike! All of us!

MRS. BILLINGS V.O.: All alright in there, Ms Byass?

JANE:	(*Rushing to the door*) Yes, Mr. Billings. All fine here. (*To the others*) Sssshhhh!
V.O.:	There's some water hot here ready.
ANNIE:	Swim in it, you old engine!
JANE:	Annie!!!!
V.O.:	What's that?
ANNIE:	We're changin' the world in 'ere. Join us, if you like!
JANE:	(*Desperate*) Annie, ssssshhhhh!!!!
V.O.:	Can I have a word, please, Ms Byass?
JANE:	I'll be right down, Mrs. Billings.
ANNIE:	Perhaps, you could join us up 'ere, Mrs. Billings?

CARRIE *laughs.*

JANE:	Annie, please! Carrie!
ANNIE:	Well.
NELLY:	You'll have us all thrown out, Annie Castledine!
ANNIE:	Your lot are already at the docks.

JANE *goes to the door.*

JANE:	Annie, please! You'll have us all done for…

JANE exits.

NELLY:	(*To* **ANNIE**) And why wouldn't they be?
ANNIE:	They'd be swimming if I 'ad my way.
NELLY:	Better than dying at his majesty's request.
ANNIE:	All the way to America.
NELLY:	Just like your own Charlie Chaplin.
ANNIE:	Shirkers.
NELLY:	Don't see him picking up no rifle.
NANCY:	Ladies, please!
NELLY:	*Ladies*, is it now?!
NANCY:	We must try and show a united front. All of us.
NELLY:	Sure.
DEE:	I've 'ad enough of all this. Shoutin' an that. Thought we was supposed to be helpin' out, not all this shoutin' and wot not. I'm off.
NANCY:	Dee, please. Let's just wait. Jane has got some important things to say. Organisation schedules. Just wait until she's back.
CARRIE:	Come on, Dee. We're only mixin' it up a bit. Larkin'. Don't sling it too soon.

DEE: I've 'ad enough. I got kids to feed.

ANNIE: Come on, Dee girl. Keep a smile on it. We're juss knockin' about. 'Ere Carrie, do your Louise. (*Back to* **DEE**) This'll tickle you. (*To* **CARRIE**) Go on, my girl. She'll love it.

CARRIE: Nah...

ANNIE: Go on, Carrie. Do your Louise. You want to see it don't you, Dee. Go on, Carrie. Please. For me, your old street 'and. Go on.

DEE *remains barely interested but* **ANNIE** *persists.*

ANNIE: 'Ere we go. So this is Louise – the Mary Pickford one. Have you seen it? *The Eternal Grind*? Who's seen it?

CARRIE: I seen it three times. I love it.

ANNIE: She loves it.

NANCY: Three times?

CARRIE: Three times and I'm seeing it again Tuesday week. I love it.

ANNIE: She loves it, does Carrie. Anyway, here's Louise – she's Mary Pickford's character and this is the bit where she sticks up for 'er skin...

CARRIE: Amy –

ANNIE: Amy.

65

CARRIE: That's Loretta Blake.

ANNIE: Amy's is played by Loretta Blake.

CARRIE: She's my favourite.

ANNIE: Thass Carrie's favourite. Anyway, this is when Louise sticks up for Amy in the factory. 'Cos they work in terrible conditions and there's a right old hullabaloo in there and suddenly Louise gives old Wharton a bit of 'er mind...

CARRIE: John Bowers.

ANNIE: John Bowers. She knows them all. Anyway, this is the bit when she 'as a right go at 'im. Go on Carrie, do it.

CARRIE takes the stage and acts out in melodramatic style in slightly speeded up silent movie pace as ANNIE attempts to mimic the penny piano music.

The scene: Louise stands in the middle of an imaginary Jane who is collapsed on the floor and the overbearing Wharton who stands above them. She implores him, then confronts him gesticulating to the stricken Jane.

ANNIE attempts a "posh" voice to narrate the dialogue frames.

ANNIE: "That's not the behaviour we would expect of a gentleman" –Carrie does old Wharton an' all.

CARRIE *spins around and takes on the character of the overbearing man with enthusiasm and concentration of a professional.*

ANNIE: "I don't expect to have to answer to a seamstress who doesn't know her place" – Go on, Carrie – do Jane –

CARRIE: Not yet – you 'aven't done the "dismissal bit".

ANNIE: Thass after Jane –

CARRIE: No it ain't. Do it "There's only one way to…

ANNIE: "There's only one way…" Oh yeah, thass it! Do it Carrie.

CARRIE *returns to her professional stance.*

ANNIE: "There's only one way to deal with a disobedient working girl and that's dismissal"

CARRIE *proceeds to throw herself on the floor as a pleading* **JANE** *begging that her sister should not lose her job.*

Just then **JANE** *re-enters the room.*

JANE: Right, well that's that then. (*To* **ANNIE**) I hope your happy 'cos ---

ANNIE: Hold on, this is the best bit…

JANE: That's the final warning ---

ANNIE: Never mind – this is the best bit!

JANE: I don't care about ---

CARRIE: (*Furious*) SHU' UP, YOU LOT!! This is the best bit.

JANE: You watch who your telling to shut up, young lady.

CARRIE: I'm trying to do the bit where Louise finally gets one over old Wharton, if you don't mind.

JANE: Old who?

ANNIE: Old Wharton.

JANE: What are you talking about?

ANNIE: Go on, Carrie – finish it off.

CARRIE: No, its done now –

ANNIE: Go on…

CARRIE: No, its gone off. Its popped.

JANE: What are two talking about? You've put us in a right position now with your shouting and ---

CARRIE: You've tipped water on the lot.

JANE: Well, thanks to Miss Castledine, we'll have to abandon the evening's proceedings.

NANCY: Nonsense. We've not even –

DEE: Thank God for that –

NELLY: Well done to the flappers in the room.

ANNIE: (*To* **NELLY**) Sing us some more blarney. (*To the rest*) You lot don't know what you're missing. You're missing the whole show. One 'alf an' black an' she does it in the noddy.

NANCY: Please, Annie! That is enough. Enough.

ANNIE: An' enough from you, lady muck! Short of staff, are you? Don't go orderin' us about.

NANCY: Nobody's ordering anybody about. We've got to find some common ground and move forward. Please.

JANE: Too late. Mrs. Billings is set to call the police if there's so much as a peep up here.

NELLY: Roll it in, Jane.

JANE: Mrs. Billings' is set...

NELLY: Fuck Mrs. Billings. We're here.

JANE: Nelly...

NELLY: We're here. Now.

JANE: (*Seriously*) Look! Are you ready? There isn't much time.

NELLY:	Are you with us?
DEE:	Us?
CARRIE:	Who's us?
JANE:	Are you ready 'cos we're doing it.
NANCY:	What do you mean, Jane?
JANE:	I mean if you lot are not game for this… you need to go now.
NELLY:	But if you're prepared to make a stand and get things moving.
JANE:	Make a change…
ANNIE:	Thass why we're 'ere, ain' it?
JANE:	There's no time for games and sing-a-longs. This is what we've been waiting for. Planning for.
CARRIE:	Who's we?
JANE:	(*Solemnly*) The Organisation.
CARRIE:	The organisation?
ANNIE:	The organisation of what?
JANE:	The Organisation of United Women Munition Workers.
NANCY:	A union?

JANE:	It's small. A coming together of like-minded people. Women. But there's other workers from other factories connected. Merryville are with us. Thaxtons in Nottingham, two in London – Claybridge and Glynns in Isleworth, Southampton's with us and more.
CARRIE:	How do you know?
JANE:	Communications.
DEE:	Communications?
ANNIE:	Don't let Paddy know – she'll be up the Post Office no time.
NELLY:	If I go for you, Annie Castledine --- you'll remember it.
CARRIE:	Ease up, bogger! Bulldog'll be there, don't you worry.
ANNIE:	We'll 'ave the lot of you swimmin' 'cross the river. You 'n' yer Fenian mates.
NANCY:	Jane, what's been decided?
JANE:	I need to know who's with us? I NEED TO KNOW WHO'S WITH US? If you're not, go now. We've no time for shirkers. We know we're just as important as the men in the trenches. We've seen the photographs of what our shells are doing over there. We

don't need any more books from the old Welsh wizard telling us the job we're doing. We know without us it grinds to a halt. If we man the same cranes, belt the same capstans, then we deserve the same pay...

CARRIE: An' we can do the same as the setter ups! It ain't all that! I could do that. I seen how they makes it look 'arder than it is. Old Johnny Sparks makes me laugh with 'is serious face givin' me the old puff puff puff this is man's work darlin' you wouldn't understand. Chuckle on. Under the machine fiddlin' with 'is nuts 'n' bolts, 'uffin' 'n' puffin'. Don't fool me – I know what your fiddlin' with mate an' it ain't as hard as you think.

ANNIE: Walk on, Carrie girl. You know when its 'ard an' when its not!

DEE: You two need scrubbin'. Inside 'n' out.

ANNIE: She gets some in 'n' out, don't worry 'bout that, Dee my girl.

NANCY: Dee, we need to take a stand. We need to agree a united stance to take forward.

DEE: I don't know.

ANNIE: Dee, you been workin' your bones since you was at Glynns sewing 'n' dopin' with the rest of 'em. Suckin' that dope 'n' keeling over with the best of'em. Did they look after you then? No! Six weeks out 'cos you knew it was a wrong 'un. 'An them kiddies of yours chewin' rope. So now your 'ere with us 'n' we got to stick together. All of us. So let's stick an ear on Jane 'n' see whats wot.

DEE: Wot are we doin'? Wot are we doin'? I been ear an hour now an' I still ain't worked out what it is we're doin'. What we're 'ere for. I's told we're 'ere to make things better. All I've heard is kickin' n screamin'.

NELLY: We're here, Dee, to make sure the management, Government, Country don't take the workers for granted and use us to sustain a war that nobody wants. That the war is not being waged with the labour of exploited people.

CARRIE: All we want is fair doos!

DEE: I know all that. I've 'eard it a hundred times. What are we doin' about it? I keep 'earin' strike strike strike. But wass it mean? 'Ows it work? Nobody's tellin' me that. I'll do me bit. For us. Everyone that's workin' til their fingers bleed an' coughin' yellow death but wot are we *doin'*?

JANE: Strike me dead if any of you are not prepared for this or go running your

73

mouths. (*Beat*) We're pulling the plug at
morning tea.

Pause.

CARRIE: Pullin' the plug?

NELLY: 11am and the factory grinds to a halt.

CARRIE: The only time that Factory grinds to a halt
is when one poor slip goes in the Devil's
porridge.

JANE: 11am it all stops.

CARRIE: I'm tellin' you – that monster don't stop till
someone's in the fire or the place goes up.

JANE: The Factory shuts down at 11a.m.

ANNIE: Which bit?

NELLY: All of it.

ANNIE: Says 'oo?

NELLY: The workers.

JANE: The women.

ANNIE: How d'you know.

JANE: That's why we're here. We've all been
meeting tonight. All the sections. Janey
Bolt's crew on section four, Maudy Sutton's
lot on cranes.

NELLY: This is the start of a bigger movement towards -

JANE: Jelly Cotton's girls in detonators are with, Mave Green's shiftinghouse lot. Ozzie Jane's fitters and turners, Kerry Murphy's dump crew...

ANNIE: Wouldn't rely on them too much –

NELLY: Jesus wept, its bigger than that.

CARRIE: So where's all this lot been meetin'?

JANE: All the sections have met up tonight in private locations to rally support and to guarantee united action.

DEE: What about Ol' Mum?

JANE: Ol' Mum's with us.

ANNIE: Ol' Mum's with us? I doubt it!

NELLY: Ol' Mum's taken care of.

CARRIE: 'Ow's she taken care of?

NELLY: Never mind Ol' Mum.

JANE: She knows the work all the girls do. The sacrifice.

ANNIE: She knows we're all out, does she?

JANE: She understands our cause.

ANNIE: Does she know we're all out at 11am?

JANE: Ol' Mum knows we need to stick together and look after ourselves 'cos no one else is going to do it.

DEE: Blow me out! Will someone answer a question straight! Does she know we're strikin' an' wot not?

JANE: (*Beat*) She's not aware of specifics.

ANNIE: There you go.

JANE: She's as unhappy with things as we are.

NELLY: Look, this is what's on the table:

They want an abolition of output restrictions to guard against any reduction in piece rates, they want the use of female labour but obviously at a price and on their terms. We can meet them half way with some of these terms but we demand equal pay with any man doing the same job as us with the same output.

ANNIE: An' wot's the men doin'? Wot's their take? 'Oos talkin' to Finnegan and the setter ups and Bob Tell an' 'is lot? Foreman Jack?

Three loud knocks on a broom handle strike the floor from **MRS. BILLINGS** *below.*

CARRIE: You said they was with us. Before, din't she?

NELLY: The men are aware that we are going to take action.

NANCY: Do they support us?

NELLY: The men are with us in terms of our grievances...

JANE: Look, there isn't much time. The truth of it is that the men support us in some matters but we have areas of disagreement in term of industrial action.

ANNIE: 'Ere we go.

CARRIE: Let's 'ave it.

JANE: The men have submitted their own list of grievances and suggestions for progress.

NELLY: No need for all ---

JANE: Let's have it out. The men, their union representatives are attempting to negotiate a series of measures that jeopardise some of our agendas...

ANNIE: Like what?

JANE: (*Beat*) They want the use of (white) colonial labour to be increased and encouraged, the re-allocation of men around the country, and the re-call of skilled men who have enlisted in the army.

Silence.

ANNIE: So, basically, they want us out?

NELLY: No.

CARRIE: So, where do we fit in?

NELLY: As part of a wider picture...

ANNIE: Where we go back to sellin' flowers an' cookin' an' scrubbin' sheets for rich folk upstairs. Not for me, my girls. Not for Annie Castledine. She's 'ad 'er fill of sewin' an' shiftin' 'n' sortin'. She's on 'er way now. No lookin' back.

NANCY: Sisters and allow me to call you sisters as much as Miss Johnson may beg to differ and you might consider me some sort of spy of the management. Nothing could be further from the truth, I assure you. If you think I have anything in common with the half-men who bid to control us, you have another thing coming entirely. It seems clear to me and to us all that a moment is approaching where the livelihoods of all women in this country are at a crossroads and we have to decide whether to fight or frankly die in terms of succumbing to a social injustice as real as any put before us.

I, in my own small way, am as much a victim of prejudice as all of you. Laugh as much as you might but until women in this country are treated equally with men and are allowed to vote for change and for the people that govern them they will never be given equal rights or pay. The Americans fought a war for no taxation without representation and we women, half the population of this country of ours, accept it as if it were the natural order of things. If we, by taking this step tomorrow can send a message to management and indeed the country then by God we should take it. And let the heavens fall because by God we've earned it and by God when we've got it we shall never let it go and by God it's a fight worth having because in a hundred years from now we might have been some use to our sisters.

ANNIE: Nancy, my old mucker, you've got my vote!

Three more booms on the floor from **MRS. BILLINGS'** *broom sound out.*

DEE: Wot'l they do? Wot can they do to us?

JANE: Nothing. If we all stick together.

DEE: Stick together?

JANE:	Yes. We've all got to down tools together. And show a united front.
DEE:	An' wot if we don't?
NELLY:	Then we'll be out in a flash. All hell will descend upon us. What's the point of pretending it won't.
JANE:	My information is that everyone is with us.
CARRIE:	So, 'ow's it all work?
JANE:	The main focus is the coordination of action.
CARRIE:	'Ow do?
ANNIE:	(*To* **CARRIE**) How we all do things at the same time, Carrie luv. (*To* **JANE**) So, 'ow's it work, Janey girl?
JANE:	All sections down tools at a pre-arranged signal.
ANNIE:	Wot's the signal? Carrier pigeons? 'Ow we all gonna know?
JANE:	All sections will be coordinated by a sequence of whistles at the moment the machines are idled at 11 tea. When the maroon sounds, that's the get ready signal.
NELLY:	Heads of sections have trench whistles to signal the industrial action.

JANE: Shell Shop One, Shell Shop Two and Shell Shop Three will be coordinated by a whistleblower at adjacent despatch doors.

ANNIE: Which Shop's out first?

NELLY: It should be coordinated ---

ANNIE: 'Oo's out first?

JANE: Shell Shop Two.

ANNIE: 'Oo's section?

Beat.

JANE: Ours.

CARRIE: We're givin' the signal?

JANE: I blow the first whistle.

Beat.

ANNIE: In for a penny.

DEE: Wot if the other sections don't blow?

JANE: They will.

DEE: Wot if they don't?

CARRIE: Then we're in for it, Dee.

JANE: They'll blow.

CARRIE: Why do we 'ave to do all the whistle blowing palaver? Why don't we just refuse to go back to our machines after tea?

ANNIE: It's symbolic, Carrie. Standing by our machines. Shows 'em we're prepared.

JANE: It demonstrates to the management that we're organised.

NELLY: It also means that we know straight away if the other sections and Shell Shops are with us. And if they're not.

CARRIE: Wot, we won't know til then?

NELLY: No.

JANE: There's a chance that we won't know what the other Shell Shops have decided. Before hand. Messages will be run throughout the shifting houses before the early session.

NELLY: But there's no accounting for people losing their bottle or a few weak links in the chain.

ANNIE: Like the Murphy lot.

NELLY: They won't be bottling, for sure. They've been fighting for longer than any of you. Battling other Empires. Don't go worrying about them.

ANNIE: Thass exactly *wot* we're worryin' about.

NELLY: We're all fighting Empires here, Annie Castledine. And one day you'll realise it.

ANNIE: An' thass the day we'll all 'ave to take sides, Nelly Johnson. We'll all be in the streets and you'll 'ave to stand behind a banner.

NELLY: Look in the mirror and see what the British Empire's done for you and your like. Have a good look. You'll soon see its absolutely nothing.

NANCY: Look, I really think we have to make some decisions. We've got to come to an understanding amongst ourselves regarding the actions we are about to take. (*To* **JANE**) I suppose, Jane, that we need to see signs of support. Amongst us.

JANE: That's right. We need to know who supports this action.

CARRIE: Wot about all the other girls? Jenny Pyke an' Fran Tully's lot. An' Ducky Jakes an' all?

JANE: Fran Tully was meant to be here tonight but told me today she couldn't 'cos her mum's dicky and couldn't leave the kids. Ducky Jakes told me she'll have her girls out and that they only need the heads up first thing.

CARRIE: An' Jenny Pyke?

JANE:	She's meant to be here. I don't know why she isn't.
ANNIE:	Monkeys to Jenny Pyke! We've got enough here to give 'em a run. I tell you staight an' true I'm up. Blow the whistle an' you'll 'ave Annie Castledine by yer, Janey girl.
NANCY:	Needless to say, I fully support this action and shall be standing by my lathe at the allotted time.
JANE:	Carrie?
CARRIE:	We don't know if any of the other girls is up for this, do we? Thass the God's honest, ain' it?

Three more loud thuds from **MRS. BILLINGS'** *broom handle sound out from below.* **ANNIE** *strides over to the door and blare out...*

ANNIE:	(*Through the door*) GO AN' TICKLE YOUR ARSE WITH A FEATHER!
JANE:	Annie!!!
CARRIE:	Now you've done it, Annie.

MRS. BILLINGS *can be heared thundering up the stairs.*

V.O.:	What was that!!!???
ANNIE:	(*At the door*) Particularly nasty weather, Mrs. Billings. Particularly nasty weather.

V.O.:   Mrs Byass, can I have a word please?

JANE: No need, Mrs. Billings. We're on our way out.

V.O.:   I'll have a quick word ----

JANE: No need, Mrs. Billings! We're on our way this instant. (*Quietly desperate*) Right! Sorry to force this but we need to know... I need to know about you others. Your decisions. Carrie, the truth is there are no certainties apart from the rightness of our cause. (*To* **DEE**) Dee?

ANNIE: (*To* **DEE**) Stick one up, Livsey, Dee. An' you can still stick one up the Kaiser.

DEE: Stick one up 'em all.

ANNIE: Thass the girl. (*To* **CARRIE**) Your shout, Carrie girl?! Louise gets her fight on an' does her bit 'gainst Old Wharton. Stickin' up for wots right.

CARRIE: *Wouldn't it make your life worthwhile.*

ANNIE: Wouldn't it just.

CARRIE: (*Thrusting out her hand*) Carrie Sefton's yer girl. (*Spits in her hand*) Them's hands that's fought off a ton of evil, as it is. Fended off blows from bullying handles and belt straps an' all. An' I'm standin' up today for an end to all that an' for wot's right. We're out of the cage here an' I ain't goin' back. Tomorrow.

ALL: Tomorrow.

CARRIE *begins to sing. The others join.*

The Girls of Shell Shop Two
Away across the roaring sea the bullets flood the sky.
The guns and bombs are deafening, the shells scream from on high...

The Lights fade. End of Act One.

INTERVAL

ACT TWO

SCENE 1

The Great Factory, 7am. The next day.

The curtain rises to reveal a cavernous, iron and brick factory in darkness. Sleeping. The huge machines lie idle. Rows and rows of 75 millimetre shells stand to attention in the gloomy light awaiting orders. An echo of 'The Girls of Shell Shop Two' can be heard. Faint. Before the storm.

Downstage right, a ceilinged canteen.

Spotlight downstage centre. Enter **OL' MUM.**

OL' MUM: I counts 'em all in an' I counts 'em all out
Every one. In they clock out they clock.
An' 'ere I stand, tickin' 'em off one an' all
They're my girls, squeezin' in through steel
Cold black gates
Ol' Mum this Ol' Mum that
Yellow hair, red hair
Coughing up guts, coughing up blood
Khaki an' blue
Where's your cap? Cover them locks
Tie it up. Watch those fingers
Mind that lathe, breathe that dust
Breathe in the filth, think of them
Over there, doin' their bit

The men say you ain't welcome 'ere
In your khaki an' blue
Livin' it up
Paintin' the town
Workin' them trams
Drivin' them cabs
Runnin' the works
Turnin' them lathes
You ain't eating 'ere
Coughin' your guts
Orange n spew.

The Lord knows, the good Lord knows
They're keepin' time
Earnin' their keep
Parlourmaids an' laundry hands,
Stepwashers
Publican's daughters an' nursemaids
Charwomen, barmaids an' flower girls
Bring me your downtrodden and underused
Bring me your defeated and abused
Ol'Mum's here, with open arms
Keep you straight.

Canteen: 7am. **DEE JESSOP** *enters. She is in heavy duty, fire resistant smock, hood and goggles. She is out of breath. She leans on the door coughing and desperately gasping for breath. She manages to make her way to one of the chairs and sits trying to regulate her breathing between coughing fits. Her breathing is rasping and she wheezes when inhaling. She pulls off her* *goggles and hood. After a moment she succeeds in catching her breathe. She gets up and walks over to the tea-urn, picks up a mug and pours herself a cuppa, adds milk and three heaps of sugar and returns to the chair. A few moments later* **LIL' GINNY**, *in overalls and cap, enters. She watches.*

DEE: (*Noticing* **LIL' GINNY**) Push on, Lil' Gin.

LIL' GINNY *stands in silence.*

DEE: Push on, girl.

LIL' GINNY: I's just up finkin'…

DEE: Fink nuffin', my girl and push on.

LIL' GINNY: I seen you an'…

DEE: An' wot? There's fings you see an' there's fings you keep. An' don't go mixin' the two.

LIL' GINNY: I seen you…

DEE: You seen nuthin', my girl.

LIL' GINNY: But I seen…

DEE: Bang a hive, girl – you get stung. You push on.

LIL' GINNY: I seen you fallin', Miss Jessop.

DEE: We're all fallin' in this world, Ginny. Thass 'ow they make it.

LIL' GINNY: But you keep droppin'. I seen it.

DEE: There's a darkness in this world, girl. An' it gets so you hav' to carry on an' stick one up it an' see 'ow it fits.

LIL' GINNY: You dyin', Miss Jessop?

Beat.

DEE: Dyin'? There's clingin' to life. Thass the thread of it. Don't go breezin' on dyin', my girl.

LIL' GINNY: (*Indicating the hood and goggles*) 'Ow d'you breathe? I mean in that lot an' the fing's?

DEE: Never you mind.

LIL' GINNY: 'Ow's it work? I mean, in there?

DEE: Thass not a place for the likes of you.

LIL' GINNY: Them big eye fings. Is it the poison smoke?

DEE: Listen, young 'un. You go skippin' 'n' tumblin' in them traps an' we're all in the clouds. In there.

LIL' GINNY: But 'ows it work, Miss Jessop?

DEE: 'Ow's it work?

LIL' GINNY: In there?

DEE: 'Ow it works in there, my girl, is all the world stops when it stops in there. This shop. This factory. This world.

LIL' GINNY: It stops?

DEE: It stops, Lil' Gin. An' us wiv it.

LIL' GINNY: It stops.

DEE: Thass right.

LIL' GINNY: It stops.

DEE: (*Beginning to cough*) Remember that, an' you'll do good by yours an' us an' all.

Enter **JANE**.

JANE: Dee, what you playin' at?

DEE: Don't go beatin' it.

JANE: You're about keeling over.

DEE: No, no, no. The weather's fine over 'ere.

JANE: The weather's fine! (*Indicating* **DEE**'s *protective clothing*) What's all this?

DEE: (*Wheezing*) Wot's wot?

JANE: This? All this? Have you been arching?

DEE: Never you mind on my fings.

JANE: Dee! Have you been stretching it?

DEE: If I stretch it… If I reckon on stretchin' mine, then thass up to me.

JANE: Dee!!!???

DEE:	Roll on.
JANE:	Dee! You came straight on!?
DEE:	I told you mine.
JANE:	You've toppled on from last night straight in and staggered out here?!
DEE:	We all grease our own here.
JANE:	In the danger room?!
DEE:	(*Indicating* **LIL' GINNY**) There's little 'uns.
JANE:	Dee!!!

DEE *eyes* **LIL' GINNY**

JANE:	Look at you. You'll tumble down before we're at it. You're going up to Livesy.
DEE:	Never mind Livsey. 'E'll be under fresh 'gyptian till nine an' no mistake.
JANE:	You're going up if I have to carry you.
DEE:	You'll do nothin' of the like. I'm 'ere for our thing an' I'll stay for our thing an' don't go addin' no layer to it.
JANE:	You won't make our thing?
LIL' GINNY:	I seen gaspin', Miss Byass.
DEE:	You go to, Ginny!!!
JANE:	Go on and brush up, Ginnie Mae.

92

LIL' GINNY: But I seen her, Miss Byass. Heavin' an' the like. Breathin' fire, it was.

JANE: Ginny!!!

LIL' GINNY: Com' in out 'a there. The red door.

DEE: That place ain't for the likes o' you. Young 'uns still fumblin' into hands of life.

JANE: You'll slip under these waters, Dee, an' before long. An' then where will you be? Dee!?

DEE: When you got seven mouths to feed, I'll put me arm around.

JANE: I've got open chirpers as well, Dee. So don't go giving me any of your bleeding heart.

DEE: I'm 'ere cos I'm 'ere!!!!!!! Don't get no fiddler playing no lament over my 'ead. I said Id be 'ere an' 'ere I am. An' don't go givin' me no sick bay. I'm 'ere cos I'm 'ere!!!

JANE: All right, Dee. All right. I'm just trying to look after ----

DEE: Look after seven bleetin' lambs first.

JANE: All right, Dee.

Beat.

DEE: You 'eard anythin'? You know, from the other lots? Jelly Cotton an' that?

93

JANE:	Not yet. I'm doing the rounds in a mo'.
DEE:	You 'aven't seen any of 'em? Ozzie Jane, none of 'em?
JANE:	Not yet, Dee. They're not in yet.
DEE:	So, we're in the dark as it is?
JANE:	Nobody's in yet.
DEE:	As it stands?
JANE:	I haven't been round yet.
DEE:	But as it stands. As it stands. It's just us?
JANE:	Dee, let's just give it a little time. Its not even seven yet.
DEE:	Keep me on board. You keep me on board an' let me know wots wot.
JANE:	I will.
DEE:	Don't let me go jumpin' overboard.
JANE:	I won't, Dee. Don't worry.
DEE:	I'm 'ere cos I'm 'ere.
JANE:	I know. Dee.

Enter **ANNIE CASTLEDINE**

ANNIE:	She 'ere?
JANE:	Who?

94

ANNIE:	Edith Cavell. 'Oo do you think? Carrie, o'course. The Deptford wildcat 'erself.
JANE:	No.
ANNIE:	Thass queer itself. Never known 'er to miss one.
JANE:	What do you mean?
ANNIE:	Twenty minutes I waited an' not so much as an 'ow do yer.
JANE:	Where?
ANNIE:	Number 27. 'Ad to get off at Crest Road 'cos thass 'ers. Waited an' waited. Nothin'.
JANE:	You were meeting Carrie this morning?
ANNIE:	An' every mornin', Jane, my girl. Every mornin'. I'm on Fleet Crescent an' she's on Crest. Tickety tock set your watch. I see 'er pearlies as we come round Woodville an' on she pops. That rare it was, I popped off to 'ang on for 'er. Two buses I waited an' not so much as a cuckoo from 'er.
JANE:	*Every* morning?
ANNIE:	Every morning. Rain or shine. Set your watch to 'er.
JANE:	Your early, aren't you?

ANNIE:	We did God's we'd be in early for the big doo dah.
JANE:	Well, that's it! She's missed a beat and forgot.
ANNIE:	Carrie Sefton? Miss a beat? Not on yours.

And **LIL' GINNY**, *always watching. Listening.*

LIL' GINNY:	Pardon me, miss.
ANNIE:	'Ere's one bright an' early on the iron brazer.
LIL' GINNY:	I's 'opin' to settle on you, Miss Byass.
JANE:	Go off, Ginny.
LIL' GINNY:	You said I'd have a little word. If you please, Miss Byass.
JANE:	Not now, Ginny. I'll find a mo –
LIL' GINNY:	If you please, Miss Byass. I got a matter wot needs sortin' apropo of things so to speak.
ANNIE:	*Apropo of things*, is it? Well, la di da, Miss Byass. Better get to.
JANE:	I'm sure we'll find a moment, Ginny.
LIL' GINNY:	But I got the early bird to see you. If you don't mind, miss. An' you said.
JANE:	All right, Ginny. What is it?

LIL' GINNY *stares at* **DEE** *and* **ANNIE**.

JANE: Don't worry about them.

ANNIE: We're all workers 'ere, Lil' Gin. End to end cozers.

JANE: Wot is it, Ginny?

LIL' GINNY: Well, Friday week wos me fourth week a workin' an' once again I goes to collect me earnin's an' once again I'm short. Four weeks in a row. 15 shillings wos wot I signed on for per week an' I keep getting 12 an' 6. See, I 'ave to give me mum 10 shillings a week so it's only leavin' me 2 an' 6.

ANNIE: 2 an' 6, can you even fink it!

DEE: For little 'uns.

JANE: All right, Gin an' what?

LIL' GINNY: Well, the fing is, me mum'll skin me if I giv 'er less an' she'll skin me if she finks I'm codgin' it somewhere.

JANE: Ginny, can we settle this…

LIL' GINNY: But it's 'ardly enough for me fares an' like. So, I went to see Ol' Mum an' she said if I didn't know wot wos wot now I soon would.

ANNIE:	I'll tell you wot's wot in a mo', Gin. You get on sweepin'. (*Quietly*) Jane, my girl, 'ow's it fallin'?
JANE:	We're on to raise it up.
ANNIE:	As one?
JANE:	It's on the table.
LIL' GINNY:	Miss Byass...
JANE:	Heavens above, Ginny! What is it?
LIL' GINNY:	If you please, Miss Byass...
JANE:	What?!
LIL' GINNY:	Its just that 'Ol Mum said read the note 'bout stoppages each week on the shiftinghouse wall.
JANE:	Yes.
LIL' GINNY:	She's says I'm taken down on loan of overalls 'n' cap, an' Christmas fund, an' lavatory cleanin'....
JANE:	That's right, Ginny. That's the same for everyone. We all get docked the same.
LIL' GINNY:	Thass all well an' good, Miss Byass but the fact of it is I done the lavvy twice an' not 'ad an ha' penny. An' 'orrible it wos, an' all – why ladies, such as they are, can't hit the pot, I don't know.

ANNIE: Never mind, kahsi cleanin' and sweepin' up, they dockin' you for the annual outin' an' chistmas party. Never mind all them other fings, Ginny girl. Its all for the big knees ups an' wot a proper time they are.

LIL' GINNY: But me mum is expectin' 'er ten shillings... I's finkin' of askin' for shifts in the danger room.

ANNIE: That ain't for you, my girl. One drop o' that porridge in the wrong place an' they'll 'ear it in France.

LIL' GINNY: 'Ow d'you mean, Miss Castledine?

ANNIE: Never you mind, my girl.

DEE: The 'ole place stops in there.

ANNIE: You move on, girl. Janglin' round here.

LIL' GINNY: I ain't janglin'.

ANNIE: Well, you push on and get them aisles brushed.

JANE: And get them buckets filled.

LIL' GINNY *exits.*

ANNIE: Danger room! She'll 'av the roof off an' us all in the ground.

DEE: Lettin' the young 'uns near there, it ain't right.

JANE: Never mind the red door. She'll be away from there.

NELLY *enters.*

NELLY: Who's here?

JANE: Morning, Nelly.

ANNIE: 'Arry Tate's Marchin' Band.

NELLY: We've enough of you, Annie Castledine.

ANNIE: 'Av another spud, trotter.

NELLY: Where's the other cockney screecher?

JANE: Carrie's is late but she'll be here.

ANNIE: Don't worry 'bout Carrie Sefton. She stands 'er part.

JANE: We're just waiting on Nancy.

NELLY: I wouldn't hold your breath on that one.

JANE: She'll be here.

NELLY: Don't count on it.

JANE: She'll be here.

NELLY: Where d'you think she was last night?

ANNIE: With us.

JANE: She'll be here.

NELLY: If you think she was straight home, you'll be laughing.

JANE: Nancy will be here.

NELLY: Well, we won't be on our own.

JANE: No.

NELLY: We've got help.

JANE: Yes. There'll be --

NELLY: Stone Legg is with us.

ANNIE: Stone Legg?

NELLY: He's coming in to set things straight.

ANNIE: Set things --?

JANE: Did you inform Stone Legg about our actions this morning?

NELLY: Stone Legg is our validation.

ANNIE: (*To* **JANE**) 'As she been gassing 'round town?

JANE: Nelly, you didn't go talking after our meeting?

NELLY: I got us what's needed.

ANNIE: (*On* **NELLY**) You never know what side them lots on.

NELLY: If you think Lady Nancy Full Of It went straight home and didn't go upstairs to tip them off of events ongoing then... well... go to sleep little baby.

DEE: You breath in that bile, Nelly Jonson. If you've somethin' to say you say it right. You say it clear. We ain't 'ere for the like of you. We're 'ere for them in hell over there. Drownin' with blood in their eyes. Drownin' for us.

JANE: Nelly! What's Stone Legg to do with anything?

NELLY: He's with us. He's coming down to discuss matters. To cement things. You think that they'll settle back and listen to the likes of us? We've to bring them to their knees. As one. Workers unite. Against *them*.

ANNIE: Them? 'Oos them. Thass *you* for me, my lagan love. Thass *you*.

JANE: What is it you've said? Black and white. What it is you've sat with Stone Legg on?

NELLY: He's coming. For unity. He's coming to negotiate terms and let us in.

From afar, factory girls can be heard singing.

ANNIE: *In*? In *wot*? In *where*?

NELLY:	You've a head on you, Annie Castledine but there's nothing in there but sawdust and jellied eels.
ANNIE:	There's enough in 'ere to know wots wot, don't you worry.
JANE:	Nelly, what is it you've been saying?
NELLY:	Stone Legg is going to sort ----

OL' MUM *enters.*

OL' MUM:	Mrs. Byass!
ANNIE:	Blimey, here's thunder.
OL' MUM:	Wot's that, Miss Castledine?
ANNIE:	Nothin' Mum.
OL' MUM:	Keep it that way, I think is best, girl.
ANNIE:	Righto.
OL' MUM:	Mrs. Byass. A word.
JANE:	Certainly.
OL' MUM:	We'll go to my ----
NELLY:	No need, Mum. We're together. All of us.
OL' MUM:	You're a party to this, are you, Miss Johnson?
NELLY:	We're united, Mum.

OL' MUM:	'Course you are, my girl. 'Course you are. (*To* **ANNIE**) An' you?
ANNIE:	We're getting things done, Mum.
OL' MUM:	Right you are. Dee Jessop? You?
DEE:	I'm 'ere 'cos I'm 'ere.
OL' MUM:	All right. Fair do's. I know what your about. All o' you.
	The water's been bubblin' a while now but 'ear this.
JANE:	Sorry, Mum but has someone been ---?
OL' MUM:	Ol' Mum's been 'ere since before time, my girl. Nothin' passes 'er. Nothin'. Unless its goin' out them gates. An' not comin' back. Nothin' comes or goes under 'er whiskers. The good Lord above 'as put 'er 'ere to watch over 'is flock an' thass wot she does. She's the light 'ere. The way. The come an' go. 'Oo thinks otherwise best come see Ol' Mum an' parley. Now, comes a time, now 'n' then when the woods get a bit misty 'n' people lose their way. Start 'eadin' to the banks o'stream yonder. The dark tumblin' stream, surgin' 'n' pullin'. An' they slip into those dark waters. 'Fore they know it, that currents taken 'em. Soon, they're in the wild ocean clingin' on to anythin' that keeps 'em bobbin' above them waves.

Keepin' themselves from goin' under. An' thass wots 'appened 'ere. A few people 'av slipped into the stream an' its taken them down to the wild sea where they're strugglin' to keep afloat. To get back to dry land. To scramble back to where they was. (*Beat*) Well, I'm tellin' you... you *can* get back. Ol' Mum's been put 'ere to guide His flock towards the safety of the shore. The good Lord above sees our moments of weakness an' doubt, juss like Peter 'oo 'ad 'is moment of doubt. But 'e saw the light an' wos forgiven as all God's children will be. Now, if Ol' Mum starts to 'ear that there's those 'oo seek to disrupt his way. 'Oo want to bring a storm down an' bring disorder to His flock. Then. Then. Ol' Mum is 'ere to do 'is biddin'. Get 'is flock rounded up 'n' back together. So now, time 'as it that Ol' Mum gets to 'ear about some girls strayin' a while an' getting' lost. Start 'avin' meetin's about certain things when they should be comin' to Ol' Mum. She's 'ere to keep them machines oiled 'n' tip top. Keep the Shop runnin' smooth. So when she 'ears that things are out of joint, where parts are scrapin' together 'causin' friction and discord, she's there to guide.

NELLY:	Well, that's all well and good, Mum. But the workers are suffering despite your good Lord's help.
OL' MUM:	The Papists often lose their way.
NELLY:	I'm no Papist, for sure.
OL' MUM:	You've slept in the same bed.
NELLY:	For God' sake ---!!!
OL' MUM:	No need to call on him when 'es 'ere with us.
JANE:	Please, you're mistaking our fight.
OL' MUM:	A fight is it? I'm mistakin' nothin'.
JANE:	We're trying to make things right.
OL' MUM:	By disruptin' the machinery? You pull them girls down, you bring it all crashin' down.
NELLY:	They've a right to be treated ----
OL' MUM:	They've a right to nothin'! Same as everyone! Ain't no such thing as right. Right? Fairness? Words for fools, do gooders an' politicians. Talk to me about rights. Right's wot you make it. 'Ow you carry yourself. The things you do an' 'ow you keep you 'n' yours. It don't come from nowhere else an' it don't come from outside.

It's wots within'. Keep your own house clean an' don't go worryin' about anybody else's. Carry yourself. There it is.

NELLY: And that's why we're where we are in this world. *Keep your own house clean.* Don't go talking about suffering and pain and injustice. Just stick in your own house and don't look out the window and see that it's the likes of you convincing poor young idiots to take what's given them every day of their God forsaken lives.

ANNIE: It's nearly clockin' on. The other Shops'll be crankin' up soon. (*To* JANE) I'll go an' see wots wot, shall I? Janey girl?

OL' MUM: I'll be tellin' you wots wot, Annie castledine.

ANNIE: Janey girl?

JANE: Why don't you see if Carrie's in.

ANNIE: She ain't. I told you ---

JANE: She might be now. Fagging up at the gate.

ANNIE: Faggin' up?

JANE: Fagging up.

ANNIE: Right you are. Faggin' up. Thass the one. (*Exiting*) I'll be juss checkin' if ol' Carrie's faggin' up at the gate.

OL' MUM: (*To all*) You watch where you're takin' them girls. 'Ol Mum's the in an' out 'ere.

NELLY: They're not going anywhere. They're here to stand on the same good earth as everyone else.

*We see **ANNIE** walking through the factory having exited from the canteen door. The factory floor is beginning to fill up with overalled girls and women chatting in twos and threes, checking gauges and testing lever handles. Some rearranging their hair under hats. As **ANNIE** moves upstage down one of the long roads between the machine. Spotlight.*

ANNIE:

> Don't you worry 'bout, Annie Castledine
> She takes it as it comes, does she.
> Rougin' it up, skippin' along
> Never you mind what's on her mind.
> We're on our way, stickin' together
> This factory ain't seen the day.
> They ain't men in our way
> They're bits of stewed string
> With all their guts sucked out
> We ain't goin' back, we're movin' on
> We're pullin' the plug
> These roarin' machines'll grind to halt
> We're standin' by our lathes
> We're makin' our demands
> Equal rights. Equal pay

NANCY LONGDON *appears, walking towards her down the road.*

ANNIE: Blimey! Where you bin? It's all goin' lopsided in there.

NANCY: Morning, Annie. What are you talking about?

ANNIE: Ol' Mum's got Jane and the ol' turf hurler over a barrel in there.

NANCY: Where?

ANNIE: Canteen.

NANCY: What's she saying?

ANNIE: Someone's let the cat out o' the bag.

NANCY: Any of the other crews in there? Mave Green? Ozzie Jane?

ANNIE: Juss our lot an' minus Carrie to boot.

NANCY: Where's Carrie?

ANNIE: She ain't 'ere an' I'm sure I don't know why. (*Beat*) I don't mind sayin' this for sport but 'ole spud runner thinks you're the rotten fish o' the catch.

NANCY: Does she?

ANNIE: An' Nelly's got Stone Legg wiv his snout in the trough.

NANCY:	Bob Legg?
ANNIE:	An' his stone face wiv 'im.
NANCY:	Did she say why?
ANNIE:	Workers unite. Bring down the management and the 'ole Empire to boot.
NANCY:	I'm sure.
ANNIE:	All we are to Stone Legg is walkin' jelly bags.
NANCY:	You're not far from it, Annie. A particularly unpleasant individual.
ANNIE:	Full o' piss!
NANCY:	Quite. (*Beat*) Annie, go back in there and get Jane to come out so I can assess the situation, would you?
ANNIE:	But I juss come out.
NANCY:	Say something. Make it up.
ANNIE:	I juss done that to get out.
NANCY:	She might need help in there.
ANNIE:	Well, Ol' Mum'll thinks somethin's…
NANCY:	We're at a critical moment, Annie.
ANNIE:	Righto, I'll do me best.
NANCY:	Quick as you can.

ANNIE and **NANCY** *exit in opposite directions. Downstage in the canteen* **DEE** *and* **NELLY** *look up at the clock and exit.* **JANE** *is left alone on stage. Sings to herself…*

For Your Daughters

My dears,

The weather's fine here – is it still bitter where you are? I wish that I could see you…

JANE *looks up at the clock and exits.* **LIL' GINNY** *enters and sees* **DEE**'*s goggles left on the equipment chest. Slowly, she goes to pick them up, then suddenly, the factory surges into life.*

SCENE 2

The Great Factory, 10. 45am (by the big clock).

The lights brighten to reveal a churning, surging factory bursting with expanding and contracting machines. A cacophony of metal clashing and pistons compressing air and steam rising from rivets being pressed and wrenches locked and turned. An ebb and flow of whirring leather belts whizzing and jolting accompanied by women cranking wheels and turning huge keys and handles. Other women wrestle and heave low slung trucks laden with immense 75 millimetre shells 12 a piece along grey wooden aisles. Rows and rows and rows of 75 millimetre shells stand to attention in columns of hundreds in forty lanes. Confident women suspended from the roof on cranes glide above them oblivious to the chaotic whirring and bubbling of the machines, they navigate on air attached to foot levers and paddles gesticulating a code of efficient sign language to each other. Their screams and shouts of procedure and alignment sound off as silent warning and advice to those on the ground. White-capped women embrace the shells, some pouring from vast containers of smoking fluids, others screwing great detonator caps on shells, others hammering down fixed powder with rubber mallets sweat bleeding from their brows. The women are part of the efficient machine, flesh and blood and hard metal and poison, holding their own in the inferno of the immense production line. Women with buckets wrist signs on the shells with yellow strokes determining their destination. The air horn clamours for attention over the chaos to signal a new batch of human carnage ready for despatch. Always the dull roar of machinery.

Projection on back wall: **Motive for Work: Patriotism. A munitions worker is as important as the soldier in the trenches, and on her his life depends.**

In one section of the factory **JANE, NANCY, ANNIE, DEE, NELLY** and **LIL' GINNY** *along with other women can be seen operating their lathes and machines with concentrated dexterity. The girls look around noting* **CARRIE**'s *absence. After some time,* **CARRIE** *enters, head down and bends straight into her machine work.* **ANNIE** *focuses her gaze on* **CARRIE.**

ANNIE:	You all there?
CARRIE:	Set and straight.
ANNIE:	Set an' straight an' eyes full ahead?
CARRIE:	On the horizon straight an' blue.
ANNIE:	There's my girl. (*Beat*) You go under a beat or two?
CARRIE:	I never did.
ANNIE:	No? 'Cos I's on Crest.
CARRIE:	An' so's I.
ANNIE:	Was you? On Crest?
CARRIE:	On Crest – I just told you.
ANNIE:	On Crest, you sayin'? Bright an' early as we done God's?
CARRIE:	I looked about but I couldn't see ya.

113

ANNIE: No? On Crest, you're saying?

CARRIE: Top deck.

ANNIE: Top deck, was it?

CARRIE: You leanin' on this?

ANNIE: Carrie Sefton says she was janglin' on Crest an' lookin'. Top deck. Fair doos. (Beat) Only I was there. An' six up easy.

CARRIE: So was I.

ANNIE: On the 27?

CARRIE: All on.

ANNIE: 27 an all easy... is wot u's sayin'?

CARRIE: I juss said it, din't I?

ANNIE: That you did. Only that ain't 'ow it was an' you know it.

CARRIE: Listen up, Annie, 'cos you're peggin' it up 'ow it ain't.

ANNIE: 'Oo's been turnin' your 'ead, Carrie?

CARRIE: No one.

ANNIE: Someone's turned your 'ead.

CARRIE: No one's done nuthin' of the like.

ANNIE: No? We're skippin' down Fawley, half 'n' black here 'n' there, all peachy at ten, doin'

Gods on this 'n' that. An' then... Who've you parleyed wiv' after that?

CARRIE: If I tell you again, Annie Castledine, it'll be too soon.

Lights up on **NANCY** *and* **JANE** *working their machines.* **DEE** *works ahead, focused, determined.* **LIL' GINNY** *watching, listening.*

NANCY: Jane...

JANE: Nancy?

NANCY: Might I have a quick word?

JANE: Now?

NANCY: Yes.

JANE: What is it, Nancy?

NANCY: (*Nodding towards* **DEE**) Are there provisions?

JANE: Eh?

NANCY: Are there things in place... "in the event". For Dee?

JANE: She'll be seen through all right.

NANCY: But if our action... isn't successful?

JANE: We'll work it.

NANCY:	I'm sure. My concern is how long can she stay afloat?
JANE:	We'll focus on this when... after the action.
NANCY:	My point is... if they should cut us off. Is there something in place?
	For the children. All the children

Lights snap back to **ANNIE** *and* **CARRIE**

ANNIE:	'Oo's turned your 'ead?
CARRIE:	Keep that neck in, Annie.
ANNIE:	Wot's done you, Carrie?
CARRIE:	There's other fings in this.
ANNIE:	We done Gods.
CARRIE:	There's other fings.
ANNIE:	There's other fings?
CARRIE:	We're all on it 'ere, you know. An' we could all go over.
ANNIE:	An' so we could.
CARRIE:	This ain't no last rose of summer, Annie. We're right in it. An' we could go over.
ANNIE:	An' we go an' wot?
CARRIE:	An' thass that.

ANNIE: Someone's 'ad you an' I know 'oo.

CARRIE: Where are we after all this? When the fog's lifted?

ANNIE: Don't you listen to her. She'll have you under the table.

CARRIE: Annie, this ain't no trippin' up an' giggling' round the back. This is the ragin' sea an' we ain't comin' back. Not 'ow we was before.

ANNIE: We're cozers, Carrie. An' always av been.

CARRIE: We go under, we ain't comin' up. Thass it.

ANNIE: Or we come up an' see land, my girl. An' it's a better land. For us all.

Light snap to **JANE** *and* **NANCY**

JANE: We'll look to our own. No one will go hungry.

NANCY: I'm sure. I've made some enquiries, Jane.

JANE: Enquiries?

NANCY: Yes, "in the event" enquiries.

JANE: Get to it, Nancy.

NANCY: There's a committee. I've made some enquiries. It's a foundation that offers help. And I think Dee might qualify.

JANE: What sort of foundation?

NANCY:	One that offers help for people in this sort of need.
JANE:	For the kiddies?
NANCY:	Yes.
JANE:	Who might find themselves on their own?
NANCY:	That's it.
JANE:	Either financially or...?
NANCY:	Yes. (*Beat*) I don't think, even in the most positive of lights, we can expect it to be too much longer. However things might transpire.
JANE:	No.
NANCY:	Obviously, it's better from you. I thought you might want to perhaps...
JANE:	How does it work?
NANCY:	I've made enquiries. She would have to come in and be... she would have to be interviewed, of course.
JANE:	Of course.
NANCY:	But it would mean things were in place if things should take a turn for the worse.
JANE:	Yes.

NANCY: I just thought it might be more… prudent for you to… broach the matter.

JANE: Thank you, Nancy.

JANE looks over at DEE set focused on her work. Lights snap back to carrie and Annie

CARRIE: D'you know wot they can do? D'you know wot's up for us on this? They'll bring the 'ole lot down on us. Not just out them gates but right out the world. They'll bring it down on us. It don't matter 'oos turned me or nuthin'. The twilight won't be gleamin' for us as we'll be in the dark. All of us. D'you know wot they can do? To us? They can round us up. All us. "Capital Offence" it is. Not just downin' the factory – it's downin' all of it. The war effort. The country. They'll come down on us like heaven come down. I've heard it all an' know wots wot – they can take us down soon as. Thass prison, Annie, an' all the way down.

ANNIE: Thass right, my girl. An' thass how it should be.

Lights up on NELLY and JANE working their machines. NANCY is behind them operating her lathe. LIL' GINNY to one side

JANE: All set?

NELLY: All set.

JANE: Following on

NELLY: We'll get the word.

JANE: Never mind the word.

NELLY: We'll wait for the word.

JANE: We go on the signal.

NELLY: Wait for the word.

JANE: We'll wait for no word from any man on this earth. If Stone Legg was with us, we'd know by now.

NELLY: He'll be here.

JANE: We go on the signal.

NELLY: They're with us.

JANE: The day I see Stone Legg and his with us is the day the world turns on its head. He looks after his own so don't go waiting on him.

Lights snap back to **ANNIE** *and* **CARRIE**

ANNIE: This ain't a lark no more. We're here. The traps open and the game's on. We started this an' we took it on an' we went wiv it an' 'ere we are. There's cozers out there – true 'n' good – 'oos comin' together an' we goin' to get fings done. All of us.

CARRIE: We'll all go back to 'ow it was. 'Ow we all was.

ANNIE: There's no goin' back.

CARRIE: I got money, Annie. First time in my rotten, stinkin', miserable life. I got metal in me purse, coppers in me palm, a weight pullin' me down an' it ain't the world. It's money, Annie. I'm livin', Annie – first time under these grey skies. Livin'. I come out of 'ere, first time in me life – I take me time. Pop in'ere, pop in there. No one tellin' me do this do that. Stop in this place, take in that, pull in the pictures...

ANNIE: (*Taking* **CARRIE**'s *face in her hands*) You can 'av that an more, Carrie. You can 'av the world. It's for all us. An' we got to take it together. All of us together. Else they'll take it back off us. An' we can't let 'em 'av it back if we get it. 'Cos it ours an' we can't let it go when we got it. An' now's our chance. So, I need you wiv us, Carrie. I need you to stand wiv us – wiv me. An' we'll do it together. All cozers together. You stick wiv me, girl. You stick wiv your Annie.

CARRIE: Yes.

ANNIE: You stick wiv your Annie, girl.

CARRIE: Yes.

ANNIE: Til it all comes down.

CARRIE: Yes.

ANNIE: Thass my girl.

Lights up on **JANE** *and* **DEE**

JANE: (*Moving over*) Dee? Dee, are you set for the road?

DEE: The travellin's hard but we're here, ain't we?

JANE: Dee, at home?

DEE: We see to our own.

JANE: Dee, listen to me. Have you got things in order? At home?

DEE: This new day's comin', ain't it?

JANE: It's coming.

DEE: You won't let me go over. You said it.

JANE: I did.

DEE: Wen that whistle blows.

JANE: Yes.

DEE: If they're goin' round takin' names, I'm 'ere.

JANE: I know, Dee. Are things in order back home?

DEE: Keep to yours.

JANE: Dee, you tell me straight. Don't go mixing me. You tell me straight, girl. You got the line covered or not? For them kiddies? Dee?! We're on the edge here, now and I got to know. You levelled it for them if it goes under? Dee?!

DEE: I done wot needs to be done.

JANE: You got a nana on? Who's covering them steps? You got skins? Dee, there's no time for this. We're on it. Its coming on. This could tip either way, girl. Who's got them kiddies?

DEE: (*Into* **JANE**'s *eyes*) You take my girls.

JANE: What?!

DEE: You take my girls, Jane.

JANE: Take them?

DEE: I got two still giddy. You take 'em, Jane. My girls.

JANE: Dee...

DEE:	You take 'em, Jane. You take 'em. I got some snugged away. Under the mattress tween the linin' and spring – a pocket. I got some in there. Enough to keep breathin'.
JANE:	Dee...
DEE:	You take 'em, Jane. An' you giv 'em love.
JANE:	Dee, please...
DEE:	You take 'em and wen my boy's are back they'll come settle. You do it for me. I'm 'ere cos I'm 'ere. For our fing. But you do this for me.
JANE:	Dee, I got my own lambs. Yearnin' every day.
DEE:	Look in my eyes and see goodnight.
JANE:	There's a new tomorrow, girl.
DEE:	You see my girls see it.
JANE:	Dee...
DEE:	The deep sea's comin', Jane.
JANE:	We ain't going under, girl. Whistles'll blow.
DEE:	We'll see the day. But wen the rattlin' comes, you see to 'em.
JANE:	Dee, we'll...

DEE: Dee Jessop's 'ere an' blow or no blow she's laid 'er cards. But take them young 'uns. Just them sucklin' two, the rest'll do. Jane, you tell me my watch's covered. Wen the rattlin' comes.

JANE: Dee...

DEE: Wen the rattlin' comes?

JANE: Yes, Dee.

DEE: You'll see my stone's kept clean?

JANE: Yes, Dee.

DEE: Wen the rattlin' comes?

JANE: When the rattling comes, Dee.

OL' MUM *appears on the gantry above. Cold. Stern. Watching.*

OL' MUM: Oh, my girls. Oh, my girls.
See how they shine, my girls.
Workers in the filth
Toilin' in the smoke
Suckin' in fumes
Brushin' off the swarf,

The wind's blowin' cold
Leadin' them away
They don't know
They can't see
Givers of life

125

Cradlin' babes
Tendin' lathes.

Black-eyed men spittin' 'n' cursin'
Sayin' they ain't worth tuppence,
Gigglin' 'n' singin' 'n' smellin' sweet.
Dodd 'n' Legg 'n' Hard Steel Face
Leather Frank an' Bob Tell
Funny Jim wiv 'is ticks an' 'is shakes.
They all weep in their mother's arms
The broken boys
In the hour of their takin' down
When the church bell's moan
When the flesh is gone
When the bones are cracked.
To their mother's arms they reach
Back to the arms
Back to the breast
The mud, its said, never gives up its dead
But crack a mother's heart and smell the
blood.

Who keep's them graves clean?
Who bathes them wounds?
Boys shakin' to death
In their beds shakin' 'n' wailin'

O' Lord, make them see the light
Tell heaven, they're comin'
My girls, my band of angels

From the rib an' into the gut
Lead the way to paradise
Don't let them fall by the way
Let their souls be rested
There's a tear to fall
This story ain't written
It's told in the lines on their faces
In the crook of their backs
In the weight of their brows
Let them live to see the day
Keep them straight
In the last mile of the way.

Projection on back wall: **One minute lost by 60 girls means the loss of one hour's output.**

NELLY: You'll lose the lot if you go down this way. You go down this way and you play into their whole game.

In the street stands **LIL' GINNY**, *listening. Always listening. Watching.*

JANE: Keep on that machine.

NELLY: Do you think Lady Whatnot's going to be standing by *her* machine? Talking committees and the like.

JANE: Nancy is with us.

NELLY: We'll see.

JANE: Nancy's with us.

NELLY: That's what they want you to believe.

JANE: Nelly!

NELLY: Her lot are for themselves.

JANE: Nelly I think...

Spotlight snaps up on **NELLY**.

NELLY: Sing a lullaby to the dying kind
John Bull kicks through the mincing machine.
Play a reel to the gallant lads
Face down in cripple creek.
Eat the hearts of the wretched ones
The wild colonial boys
Slipping under the muddy waves
Gasping for air and spitting blood.
Kitch'll have you over the cliff
Chasing shadows of other ghosts.
No milky breasts to lay their heads
All the fair and tender ladies
Are running streets and tending lathes.
The home fires are frosted blue
And night is on the hill, my boys,
Lay down your weary heads
And lets come together to fight
And bring the bastards to their knees.

Spotlight snaps down. In the street stands **LIL' GINNY**, *listening. Always listening. Watching.*

JANE: Nancy's with us.

128

NELLY: That's what they want you to believe.

JANE: Nelly!

NELLY: Sure she is.

JANE: Nelly, I think...

NANCY: (*Moving towards them*) Thank you, Jane, but I think, Miss Jonson has some superior knowledge...

NELLY: Twistin' n turnin' like the lot of you.

NANCY: Why don't you furnish us with all your information? All your insinuation.

NELLY: Where were you off to?

NANCY: Off to?

NELLY: You know, Lady Longdon. After the meeting?

NANCY: Last night?

NELLY: Last night? No, a week Friday. Course last night.

NANCY: For your information and records, I returned home.

NELLY: You're Curzon Street, aren't you? Mayfair way?

NANCY: You've had your spies out.

NELLY: You headed home, is it you're saying?

NANCY: I shan't be repeating myself, Miss Jonson. Impertinence might be a trait with your people but not mine.

Projection on back wall: **Slacking at meal and at closing time means loss of output.**

NELLY: And you've headed home is it? Walkin' down Bishop?

NANCY: Really!

The other girls begin to focus in on the mounting storm.

NELLY: Down Bishop. Out into Clerkwell.

CARRIE: Three minutes. On the clock.

JANE: Thank you, Carrie.

NELLY: And then where?

NANCY: Pardon me?

NELLY: And then where, Miss Longdon?

NANCY: I fail to…

JANE: What's she saying, Nancy?

ANNIE: Where did you go, Nancy?

NANCY: I went home, Miss Castledine. Exactly where I said I went. Before the interrogation began.

NELLY: Only it wasn't home was it? Was it?

JANE: Nancy?

ANNIE: (*Looking up at the clock*) World's up. We goin'.

JANE: All in, Annie. Nancy?

NELLY: Off home was it?

NANCY: Really.

CARRIE: Where did you go, Nancy?

NANCY: I'm not going stand here and be interrogated by –

NELLY: By the working classes who should be showing a united front against the privileged and entitled class who will never see those below them as anything but wood in their fire.

NANCY: HOW DARE YOU... HOW DARE YOU!!! INSOLENT! INSOLENT! HOW DARE YOU CROSS QUESTION ME YOU... YOU LITTLE IRISH... GUTTERSNIPE!! YOU PEASANT BIDDIE! QUESTION ME, YOU INSOLENT PADDY... BOGTROTTER!!

JANE: Miss Longdon, please.

NELLY: It's coming out.

NANCY:	I'LL HAVE YOU WHIPPED!! QUESTION ME? YOU INSOLENT MICK!!!
NELLY:	And the rest, m'lady. Let's have it all.
NANCY:	I'VE QUITE HAD MY FILL OF YOUR FENIAN BILE!!!
ANNIE:	Easy up, Nancy!
NELLY:	Here we are. The grounds been cleared now. Everything's clear and as it should be. (*To* **JANE**) Do you see? Do you see?
NANCY:	QUESTIONING ME!!!
NELLY:	That's it.
JANE:	Nancy?
NANCY:	INSURPORTABLE! REALLY?!
JANE:	Nancy?
NELLY:	There we are. When all's back to normal and the war's over, we'll back to the barricades. You'll see. No more pretending. No more horse shit equality and we're all one for the effort. Liberal do-gooders'll be buried in the mud of Flanders. And then it's us and them. We'll meet in the streets. We'll meet in the dirty alleys and the real war'll begin.

CARRIE: (*Pointing to the big clock*) It's on, Jane?! Annie!!!

JANE: Thank you, Carrie!

ANNIE: It's comin' on!

NELLY: The real war'll begin, don't you worry. Jetsam and flotsam of your British Empire. Where's all them poor bastards that's done the donkey work? Returning to their little hovels while you sip the viscount's nectar. Where's their --?

CARRIE: This is us! It's turnin' on.

JANE: Heads down, all o' you.

DEE: (*Exploding into life*) WILL YOU LOT, FOR ONE MINUTE, BRUSH YOURSELVES OFF AN' COME TO!!!!!!

A spotlight snaps on **DEE** *as the others freeze.*

DEE: (*Desperate, urgent*)
I'm here, my love, I'm here
I'll follow you, I'm yearnin' to
There's plenty here to be done
That charcoal brazer ain't got me still
There's plenty to be done
We haven't killed the Kaiser yet.
Sawn billets come in the back
We fill 'em up and bang 'em out
We're 'ere to do our bit

133

One a dump and two a scrap
Mystic on a sponge an' wipe it clean
There's plenty to be done yet
Kiss the shells and parley vous
I'll drop down dead and send 'em through
I'll keep comin' till me hands swell up
Ill keep comin' till me lungs are blood
Till me hair's on fire
Till me eyes are puffed
Till me breath is raw
Till me skin is dead
Across the sea and into the trees
My shells are comin', my darling
I'll be with you soon
For there's plenty to be done yet.

Spotlight snaps down.

CARRIE: Thass us!

JANE: Hold firm.

ANNIE: We're on.

JANE: Keep in.

Projection on back wall: **Miss Tommy Atkins, how will you answer your children when they ask you what you did for the Great War?**

CARRIE: Times alive!

JANE: Wait on the –

The piercing sound of the maroon sounds. It rises above the sound of the surging machinery. Silence. The women look at each other.

*All eyes are on **JANE**. She reaches for her overall pocket. Slowly, she pulls out the whistle. Piercing silence. **OL' MUM** looks on.*

JANE *puts the whistle to her mouth. The women go to their machines and stand by them. **JANE** lets out a call on the trench whistle that breaks the shroud of silence. The women look ahead with pride and trepidation.*

Silence.

LIL' GINNY *looks desperately at **JANE**.*

The women look on. Listening. Waiting. Nothing.

ANNIE: Blow it again, Jane!

JANE *looks at the other women. She puts the whistle to her mouth and blows. Silence. **'OL MUM** looks on.*

Silence.

JANE *puts the whistle to her mouth again and blows. Silence. The women look at each other. Some heads sink.*

LIL' GINNY: It'll stop, Miss Byass. It'll all stop.

LIL' GINNY *breaks away and runs toward the exit of the shell shop.*

*The women, slowly, achingly, begin to move away from their machines and walk dejectedly towards the canteen. **'OL MUM** looks on (smiling).*

ANNIE *and* **CARRIE** *reach the canteen door… and then…*

A whistle, far off sounds. The women stop in their tracks. From afar another whistle sounds. One nearer sounds. From afar, another. The Shell Shops respond to the call. Then a unison of whistles.

The women turn to each other.

CARRIE: They're with us. They're with us.

ANNIE: That they are, my girl.

JANE: There you are, Dee!

DEE: All of them an' us.

JANE: That's right, Dee. All of them and all of us. Together.

NANCY: The other shops…

NELLY: They're all blowing.

JANE: Every section, every shift. Every unit, every street.

CARRIE: With us.

ANNIE: With us, Carrie girl.

In the distance, echoing, women workers, sing…

WOMEN WORKERS: (*Singing*)

> In the trees, in the trees
> Outside of Shell Shop Three

The sky is coming down

JANE: We're out. All out together.

But... In the distance, the workers singing turns to screams. From afar – shouts --

VOICES OFF: GINNY, NO!!! GINNY!!! DON'T GO IN THERE...!!!!

JANE: Where's Lil' Ginny?

CARRIE: She run off...

A whooshing sound of air being sucked in. A backdraft. Followed by a sudden, blinding flash of white light. Followed by...

A DEAFENING EXPLOSION

DARKNESS

SILENCE

Sound of a projector. Pathe newsreel of women munitions workers at work on the back factory wall. Then still images with the following:

In July 1917, an explosion at the Silvertown munitions factory in East London was heard as far as Cambridge. It flattened everything in a 500 yard radius and destroyed three blocks of the East End. There were 73 deaths, mostly women, 100+ seriously injured and 1000+ minor injuries.

In July 1918, 8 tons of TNT exploded at Chilwell, Nottingham, killing 134, mostly women and injuring 250+.

The Barnbow Munitions factory, near Leeds, was destroyed on 5 Dec 1916 killing 35 women outright. There had been two previous lesser explosions killing 2 women and 3 men but these had been kept secret.

On the 13th June 1917, the Hooley Hill Rubber and Chemical Works Ashton-under-Lyne, [making TNT] Exploded 43 Killed.

A huge explosion at Faversham involving 200 tons of TNT killed 105 in 1916.

Many more deaths occurred in other explosion around Britain during the First World War.

Prolonged exposure to the chemicals also caused serious health risks for the munitionettes. Exposure over a long period of time to chemicals such as TNT can cause severe harm to the immune system. People exposed to TNT can experience liver failure, anaemia, spleen enlargement and TNT can even affect women's fertility.

The war achieved for women what years of political agitation could not. In February 1918, women over the age of 30 were given the vote, in recognition of their contribution to the war.

In 1914, the munitions industry employed 212,000 women; by 1917, the number had risen to 819,000. This represented 60 percent of all workers in the munitions industry.

Most women lost their jobs once the soldiers came home from the war. By 1920, the number of women in the workforce was less than it had been in 1914. But some had been let **OUT OF THE CAGE**. Never to return.

LEST WE FORGET

The end.

Music and Lyrics by John Chambers

SONGS

Not the Girls You Left Behind You

We're not your angels in the aisles
Not your lovelies in the streets
We can paint on pretty smiles
Or wear the yellow of our cheeks
And we're painting up the shells
And we're breathing in the filth

And we're not the girls you left behind you

We're not as helpless as you think
And we're not a damn disgrace
And we can curse and we can drink
Or just forget to know our place
And we're coughing up our guts
And we're here to do our bit

And we're not the girls you left behind you

We are mothers in a rage
We are sisters asking "why?"
We are daughters in a cage
And we can hold up half the sky
And we're here running the works
In our khaki and our blue

And we're not the girls you left behind you

Wouldn't he look handsomer in khaki?

Wouldn't he look handsomer in khaki?
Wouldn't he look fine in uniform?
Wouldn't he look grand, rifle in his hand,
Marching off and fighting up a storm?
Think of your heart swelling when you see him,
standing there with medals on his chest.
Surely it's much better than him wearing a *white feather?*
Yes, boys who dress in khaki are the best.

The Girls of Shell Shop Two

Away across the roaring sea the bullets flood the sky.
The guns and bombs are deafening, the shells scream from on high.
The aeroplanes cut through the clouds, the mines crash loud and true.
Who helped them do their job so well? The girls of shell shop two.

Our broken boys have hands of red - their trenches fill with blood:
It's British and it's German, bubbling upwards through the mud.

Their lovely eyes have turned to grey, those eyes that once were blue.
Whose yellow hands have made it so? The girls of shell shop two

The men cry for their mothers as they break against the line.

Their mothers cry then trudge the streets and make another mine.

And when more soldiers join the front and paint fresh hell anew -

Who helped them do their job so well? The girls of shell shop two.

For Your Daughters

My dears,

The weather's fine here – is it still bitter where you are? I wish that I could see you.

I wish this war were over. Please understand I'm doing this for you, and for your daughters. And in a hundred years, when we're all in the clouds, they might look up and thank us.

Listen to your grandmother. There's care and wisdom there.

All my love and hope,

Mum

GLOSSARY OF TERMS

'Alf 'n' black: Blend of pale ale and stout or porter

Banger depth: Space for correct amount of explosive in a shell

Bogger: From bogtrotter (derogatory terms for an Irish person)

C.E. work: Cordite Explosive

Clearing Sheet: Government directive that anyone leaving a munition factory cannot be re-employed in another factory for six weeks

Cozers: Mates/fellow workers

Devil's porridge: Mixture of nitroglycerin and gun-cotton

Dump shell: Faulty shell needing reworking

End to end cozers: Workers who share sleeping arrangements

Janglin': Lazy or unproductive

Jelly Bags: Munition workers' hats

Kitch: Lord Kitchener, Secretary of State for War

Meeows: (Slang) Upper class female munition workers

Mystic: Soap and water mixture used to cool machinery

NUWSS: National Union of Women's Suffrage Societies

Old Welsh Goat/Welsh Wizard: nicknames for Lloyd George

On the burst: Out drinking

Proper smart kiddies up the hill: Australian soldiers

Sawn Billets: Empty shell casings

Scrap shell: Shell casing to be melted down

Setter up: Men who prepare machines for operation

Sewin' 'n' dopin': Method of sewing aircraft fabric and then hardening them with cellulose varnish

Swarf: Metal shavings from machined shell casings

White feathers: A symbol of cowardice

Windy boys: Cowards